TAKE ANOTHER LOOK AT GUIDANCE

TAKE ANOTHER LOOK AT GUIDANCE

A Study of Divine Guidance

BY BOB MUMFORD

Edited by Jorunn Oftedal Ricketts

PLAINFIELD, NEW JERSEY

Standard Book Number: 912106–17–4
Library of Congress Catalog Card Number: 77–166498

© *1971 by Logos International*
Logos International
Plainfield, New Jersey
U. S. A.

To the Rev. Walter Beuttler,
Teacher, spiritual father, friend.
It was he who taught me principles, not methods.

Thus saith the Lord, thy Redeemer, the Holy One of Israel; I *am* the Lord thy God which teacheth thee to profit, which leadeth thee by the way that thou shouldest go.

O that thou hadst hearkened to my commandments! then had thy peace been as a river, and thy righteousness as the waves of the sea . . .

Isa. 48:17–18

CONTENTS

Two functions—Prophecy in guidance—Nine scriptural ways to judge prophecy—Giving prophecy its proper place.

A point of reference—An end in itself?—Relationship to spirituality—Spiritual scaffolding—Evaluating angelic visitors—Visions in guidance—Preparation for ministry—Warning of danger—Dreams and dill pickles —Interpreters of dreams—Dream books.

Accommodation and unbelief—Three categories of signs —The use of signs in guidance—Interpreting the signs —Inward dispositions—Counterfeit signs—Final answers—Gideon and his fleece—Second-generation skeptics—Divine displeasure—Fleeces and circumstances— Exception and the norm—Florida or California oranges?

Confidence or dependence?—Candles or sealed beams —Knowing the future—Spiritual maturity—Tunnel experiences—Feelings and guidance—The time factor— Sheep and lambs—Passing the initiative—From cocoon to butterfly—The fully guided life.

PREFACE

There are those who say that God cannot and will not guide us today. Others say loosely, "God led me . . ."

The following pages are an attempt to *Take Another Look* at guidance in the light of what the Bible teaches on the subject.

Neither God nor His Holy Spirit can be reduced to methods, but in searching the scriptural record we come to recognize that He does work according to clearly outlined principles.

This is not a theological treatise or an effort at high scholarship. I simply invite you to *Take Another Look* with me as we attempt to distinguish God's guidance from the confusion of our own desires, prejudices, preconceived notions, and impulses clamoring for our attention.

I take great comfort in the promise given us in Isa. 35:8: "And a highway shall be there, and a way, and it shall be called the Holy Way; the unclean shall not pass over it, but it shall be for the redeemed; the wayfaring men, yes, the simple ones and fools, shall not err in it and lose their way" (*Amplified Bible*).

My sincere prayer is that our journey together may contribute to your growth, safety, and pleasure along the way. Remember, no man gets lost on a straight road!

TAKE ANOTHER LOOK AT GUIDANCE

GUIDANCE ... FROM WHERE?

Have you ever wondered about your future?

Have you asked yourself: Who am I? Where did I come from? Where am I going?

Have you ever wondered about the purpose of your life?

"Sure," you say, "who hasn't?"

The questions are so basic it seems almost silly to ask them. But we've all asked them.

So where do you go for your answers?

I read an article recently in *Reader's Digest* stating that the businessmen, the politicians, and prognosticians of our generation read the charts and graphs and stock-market reports just as our forefathers used to read the entrails of the chickens.

If you've walked into a bookstore or glanced over the bookracks in the drugstore or supermarket, you've probably noticed how many books deal with one form of guidance or another: How to know your future. How to improve your power of thinking. How to seek the stars for guidance. How to open your mind to the supernatural wisdom of the universe. On and on it goes. Books on interpretation of dreams, on horoscopes, on ESP, mind reading, and how to conduct a seance. Even books on how to make witches' brews to make yourself irresistible or put a hex on your enemy.

Party games for kids and grown-ups include Ouija boards, seances, and fortune-telling.

Millions of readers study their daily horoscope in the newspaper "just for fun" or seriously before deciding on a new job, a new car, or a wedding date. Who hasn't read or desired to read "prophetess" Jeanne Dixon's predictions for the future, Edgar Cayce's books, or astrology predictions by "Dame" Sibyl Leek?

How about the batteries of tests given to every child in elementary school to determine who he is and what he'll be like in the future? Or personality inventories fed into computers to determine what job you're suited for or what kind of partner you should choose in marriage? That's looking for guidance too!

Millions of young people try various mind-expanding drugs to "find themselves." Middle-aged couples are stranded in the divorce courts. "We made a mistake," they say sadly of ten or twenty years together. "We didn't know ourselves or what we wanted in life."

So life in today's world seems a confused mess with its riots, pollution, wars, and tight economy—and the most you can do is make the best of it.

Or *is* there a right way, a meaningful purpose for your life, a right vocation, a right partner in marriage? Is there a surefire way to *know* who you are and where you're going?

The surfers use the expression "right on" to describe the perfect ride on the perfect wave. You catch the wave just right and it takes you just where you want to go. The Greeks had a word to describe the exact opposite: *hamartia*. It means "to miss the mark."

All of our strivings to find ourselves and search out our future is with a single purpose in mind. We want to be "right on." We don't want to miss the mark.

Yet most of us miss the mark because we don't know what the mark is. If we don't know where we're going, how can we get there? We are like the man who jumped into the taxi and said, "Take me there!"

The utter confusion among the seekers of truth and guidance in the world stems from the basic fact that they believe all wisdom comes from the same source.

The Bible teaches plainly that this is not so. There is a wisdom from above: from God. And there is a wisdom from below: from Satan. Both are supernatural. Both can be sought. Both can be found. Also the Bible teaches plainly that the wisdom from above is truth. The other is false. One is "right on," leading us to hit the target. The other causes us to "miss the mark."

It is possible to learn to distinguish one from the other, and the proof of the pudding is always in the eating. There are obvious and predictable results from following the wisdom from above or the wisdom from below.

The Greek word *"hamartia,"* to miss the mark, is the word translated in our English Bible as "sin." The Bible teaches that we are born sinners, unable to hit the mark on our own. But the Bible also teaches that God has made provisions for our condition. He sent Jesus Christ, His only begotten Son, to die on the cross for our missing the mark, thereby reestablishing us in a right relationship with God, our Father.

God made the *provision,* but each of us must accept it for himself. We are given the freedom of choice, and our destiny is determined by what we choose. We can accept or reject our relationship with God in Christ.

God's Word tells us that Jesus is the way, the truth, and

the life and that no one can come to the Father any other way. It also says that salvation is the undeserved gift of God, not something earned by our works of goodness. We're saved, not by our own wisdom, cleverness, or good deeds, but by faith in Jesus Christ.

We cannot even know what life is all about until we take that *first* step toward the purposes of God in our own lives. Jesus knows the answer to the age-old riddle. He declared that He knew from whence He came, who He was, and where He was going (John 8:14). It is He who desires to bring the same certainty to you.

The Apostle Paul tells us that the secret of Christianity is that Christ actually dwells *in* the believer by faith. With Jesus Christ *in* us, we can begin to focus in on what life is all about for us personally.

Now God has made a *second* provision for our guidance. John the Baptist, who baptized in water those who repented of their sins and turned from their wrongdoings, said of Jesus Christ that *He* would baptize the believer in the Holy Spirit. In the Book of Acts we read again and again that this was the common experience for the new converts to Christianity.

Peter tells the people of Israel gathered at Jerusalem for the celebration of Pentecost: "Repent, and be baptized, every one of you, in the name of Jesus Christ for the remission of sins, and ye shall receive the gift of the Holy Spirit" (Acts 2:38).

Jesus talks about the Holy Spirit in John 16:13: "Howbeit when he, the Spirit of truth, is come, he will guide you into all truth: for he shall not speak of himself; but whatsoever he shall hear, that shall he speak: and he will shew you things to come."

The Holy Spirit is a gift, a promise, and here again we are

faced with a choice: to ask for and receive it, or reject it. Again our destiny will be determined by our decision. Again our self-will is at stake. It is a question of surrendering our will and our opinion to the will of God as revealed in the scriptures.

Jesus came into our lives at the moment of salvation when we were born again of the Spirit. So we have Him as our Savior, but how much of us does He have?

Accepting Jesus Christ as Baptizer in the Holy Spirit takes us another step into God's will for us. We surrender more of our being to Him. A perfect example is found in the result of submitting the "unruly member" of our being, the tongue, to Jesus. Not only does this quench all gossip and backbiting, but it allows the Holy Spirit to give us His words to speak and pray whereby we do not have to depend solely on our own intellect. Paul speaks of this as speaking or praying "in tongues" (I Cor. 14:2,14).

The *third* provision God has made available for our guidance is His Word, the Bible. Without the Word of God it is impossible to hit the mark in our lives. It is impossible for us to know the will and the purposes of God. These must be revealed to us.

Jesus told the Jews who believed on Him: "If ye continue in my word, *then* are ye my disciples indeed; And ye shall know the truth, and the truth shall make you free" (John 8:31–32).

Again we are faced with a choice: to accept the Word of God as truth or not. Again our choice will determine our destiny, whether or not we'll hit the target and move on into God's will and purpose for our lives. Everyone lives by some authority, whether Pluto or Plato. Blessed is the man who makes God's Word to be his authority. Jesus said that if we do, we will never be put to shame!

Now let us assume that you've taken the first steps outlined for us by the Word of God. You've confessed and repented of your sins, accepted Jesus' death on the cross in your stead, and received the promise, the Baptism in the Holy Spirit. You've decided to read more in the Bible and to accept it as truth.

Surely now you've tuned in on the wisdom from above and tuned out the confusing impulses from any other source. Unfortunately, it isn't quite that simple.

Much of the confusion about guidance among Christians comes from the sad fact that we do not recognize that we are exposed to counterfeit "wisdom" which is not from God. Satan deals with both nonbelievers and believers, but he deals with each differently. John Wesley said: "Do not hastily ascribe things to God. Do not easily suppose dreams, voices, impressions, visions or revelations to be from God. They *may* be from Him, they *may* be from nature, they *may* be from the devil. Therefore, believe not every spirit, but try the spirits, whether they be from God."

The Bible promises that a child of God *can* know the perfect will of God for his life and know the joy, reality, and fullness of divine guidance. We don't want to overemphasize the danger of negative or false guidance, the Satanic counterfeit. But it is important to sound a warning at the start in order to determine what guidance is NOT.

Once a young man at the college where I taught came to me and said, "Bob, I have a wonderful form of guidance. There is a presence surrounding me. Anytime I ask a question, I receive an immediate answer from this presence."

Immediately I became suspicious and questioned the young man. It was apparent that he was involved with what the Bible calls a "familiar spirit." Having a "familiar spirit" means simply he had cultivated a relationship and become *familiar* with a spirit from the supernatural world. This spirit, as is often the case, was posing as the Holy Spirit.

I weighed this matter in my heart and asked God for discernment. Two days later the young man was in my office again and I asked him point-blank, "Have you ever been involved with witchcraft or mind reading?"

His eyes took on a strange look, as though they could see through me, and he said, "How did you know? Ever since I was a child my mother has exposed me to fortune-tellers."

Asking him to sit down, I opened my Bible and read: "There shall not be found among you any one that maketh his son or his daughter to pass through the fire, or that useth divination, or an observer of times, or an enchanter, or a witch, or a charmer, or a consulter with familiar spirits, or a wizard, or a necromancer. For all that do these things are an abomination unto the Lord: and because of these abominations the Lord thy God doth drive them out from before thee. Thou shalt be perfect with the Lord thy God" (Deut. 18:10–13).

Then I explained: "Divination means fortune-telling. An observer of the times is an astrologer. An enchanter is a genuine magician, performing not childish parlor tricks but actual works of magic. A witch is a sorcerer. A charmer is a hypnotist. A consulter with familiar spirits is a medium with a 'guide.' A wizard is a clairvoyant or psychic. A necromancer is one who consults with the dead."

As I talked the presence of the Holy Spirit became apparent in the room and a look of understanding dawned in the boy's eyes. "People use these counterfeit means of guidance to unveil hidden knowledge, ascertain future events, uncover secret wisdom, and exercise supernatural power," I said. "But you see, all this and more can be found through the Holy Spirit. Are you willing to surrender this counterfeit form of guidance for one that is genuine and biblical?"

He nodded and said he wanted true deliverance. We prayed, according to the new covenant which was provided in the blood of Jesus Christ, for release. He stepped out of my office a new man. Today he is in the ministry.

Satan has a very special arsenal of weapons which he uses against the Christian. He gets to us through superheated impulses and uncontrolled imaginations. Satan seduces, deceives, accuses, condemns. He is the master of false guidance and deception.

The key word here is, of course, deception. Satan is a liar. It is imperative for us to acquaint ourselves thoroughly with the truth of God's Word which is the antidote to lies and deceptions. Thus through the ministry of the Holy Spirit we will recognize a lie when we are required to judge. This is the armor God has provided so that we can withstand every fiery dart from Satan.

It is tragic that many misled, uninformed people have committed indescribable acts of horror and immorality and later, when questioned in court, they've said, "God spoke to me and told me to do it." They may have heard a voice, but had they *known* God as He reveals Himself through His Word, His Spirit, and His Son, they never would have believed the false guidance and acted on it.

Divine guidance is further complicated by the *trickery* of our own mixed-up emotions, our impure motives, our prejudices, and our old habit patterns of thought and action. It is at this point that some who have seen the obstacles or know of some particular or spectacular failure turn their backs in fear of a deeper commitment to God's way. Whole churches have clamped the lid on any possibility that God can speak to His children today. They say that He has spoken through His Son in the scriptures and that's that; they say all this foolishness about the Holy Spirit telling people what to do and where to go was strictly for the church of the first century; they say, "We're living in a different dispensation and don't need the supernatural divine guidance that comes through the gifts and manifestations of the Holy Spirit." These are the people who call themselves "practical Christians" and boast that they have both feet firmly planted on the ground. They accuse their more mystically inclined brethren of being "so heavenly minded that they're no earthly good."

On the other hand there are those who boast of deep mystical experiences in the realm of the Spirit and who look down their noses at the "uninitiated ones." I would like to suggest that both groups have missed the mark. While these people seem to look at the world as either natural or supernatural, the reality is that our lives are and should be a *balance* of both.

The man who chooses to live entirely in the natural thinks he is safe. He says, "By rejecting the mystical and keeping myself solidly based on the Word of God, I'll never go astray." Perhaps this holds some truth. But he will never enjoy that intimate walk with God, guided by the presence of His Holy Spirit, that the early apostles enjoyed. He may be safe, but he will be robbed of the delights that are the rewards of a more adventurous soul. *He is the careful failure.*

The twelve disciples were together in a boat at sea when Jesus came walking toward them on the water. Peter cried out, "Lord, is that You? And if it is You, bid me come." Jesus said, "Come!" Peter got out of the boat and walked on water. Yes, he did start to sink, and it was a fearful experience. But consider the eleven careful failures who remained in the boat. They didn't even attempt to walk on the water.

Peter, whose heart cried out for all that God had for him, took the risk. He made that leap of faith into a state of trusting God. Peter, the adventuresome, impulsive one who sometimes made eager promises he couldn't keep, later became the rock, the obedient, the solid one.

If you've honestly set your goal to be led of the Spirit, then you must set yourself to learn four basic principles about guidance.

First, *guidance doesn't come automatically.* You can't push a button, open your Bible at random looking for a verse, or listen for voices.

Second, *receiving guidance is a skill to be learned,* often through trial and error which will demand some spiritual adventure on your part.

Third, *receiving guidance is not a set of methods,* but is based on obedience to a set of principles.

Fourth, *guidance is intensely personal.* It is a relationship between you and your Father, God, through Jesus Christ and the person of the Holy Spirit. It is God's guidance for *your* life, and only *you* can receive it from Him.

A final word of caution: A decision to earnestly seek God's guidance and plan for our lives necessitates a clean break with all other forms of guidance. The Bible lists all attempts at seeking to know the future by any means other than the direct revelation of God, as sin, and therefore something we must confess, repent of, and turn from. This specifically includes all forms of spiritism, seances, fortune-telling, card-reading, crystal-ball gazing, astrology, horoscopes, Ouija boards, palmreading, handwriting analysis, ESP, clairvoyance, mind reading, parapsychology, science of mind religions, and other related methods.

There can be absolutely *no compromise* in this realm for the Christian, for this is precisely how the supernatural wisdom from below, Satan's counterfeit, gains access to our lives. The consequences have been tragic for those who have opened themselves to these influences: agony, despair, and mental torment, confusion, depression, and for some, at last, suicide.

In James 3 we find a clear description of the two forms of supernatural wisdom: "There is a wisdom which descends not from above, but is earthly, sensual, devilish." Other translations give you these words: "There is a wisdom that is a supernatural wisdom which doesn't come from above." It is a supernatural power which works in the same way as divine guidance. A literal translation describing the fruit of this wisdom goes like this: "But where there is a supernatural wisdom which is working which is *not from above,* but is really earthly, natural, that is, soulish, and inspired by demons, there is jealousy, rivalry, tumult, and every worthless practice."

In direct contrast is James's description of the wisdom which comes from above: "For the supernatural wisdom (the guidance, the leading of the Spirit of God) which comes from above is first pure, then peaceable, gentle, easy to be entreated (teachable, not rigid), full of mercy, without partiality, without hypocrisy, and the fruit of righteousness is sown in peace of them that make peace." *The Amplified Bible* says it is "pure (undefiled) . . . peaceloving, courteous (considerate, gentle) . . . [willing to] yield to reason, full of compassion and good fruits; it is wholehearted and straightforward, impartial and unfeigned—free from doubts, wavering and insincerity. And the harvest of righteousness (of conformity to God's will in thought and deed) is [the fruit of the seed] sown in peace by those who work for and make peace—in themselves and in others . . . that peace which means concord (agreement, harmony) between individuals, with undisturbedness, in a peaceful mind free from fears and agitating passions and moral conflicts."

As we begin to seek God's guidance for our lives, we must be willing to *submit* the impressions we receive to the test. God's Word is the final judge, and that means it *must* take precedence over our emotions, feelings, impressions, any signs or leading we've received. *God's Word must take precedence over our subjective confidence that God has indeed spoken to us in some personal revelation.*

If a revelation doesn't agree with God's Word and pass the test of James 3, our source of wisdom is not from above, and must be rejected, however convinced we are that it is "of God"!

A note of reassurance: As we grow in maturity, both in the Word and in the knowledge of our Lord and Savior Jesus Christ, we can be as sure about our guidance as we are about our salvation.

We can know the fruits of guidance and recognize that we are not being deceived. We can distinguish between the guidance of the Holy Spirit and the subtle counterfeit of Satan. We can, as well, avoid being led into a dead-end street, fruitless activities, or subjective confusion.

Rom. 8:14 says: "For as many as are led by the Spirit of God, they are the sons of God." When you allow yourself to be disciplined and trained to the leading of God's Holy Spirit you are then showing the quality of a mature son.

2

MY WAY—OR GOD'S WAY?

The danger in using familiar words is that we sometimes lose sight of their meaning. Many Christians talk loosely about the "saved" and the "sinners." "Saved" usually denotes the ones who have accepted Jesus and are on their way to heaven. "Sinners" categorizes the rest of mankind, those who have rejected Jesus Christ and consequently are condemned. Now this is such dangerous oversimplification that it leads to error.

True, acceptance or rejection of Jesus Christ as the Redeemer who died on the cross for our sins is the key to salvation and to eternal life. It must be remembered, however, that "sin" is a translation of the Greek word *hamartia*, meaning to "miss the mark." Thus if we imply that all those who have accepted Christ and are born of the Spirit have hit the bull's-eye and are fulfilling God's purpose and plan for their lives, then we need to redefine our terminology. Acceptance of Jesus Christ as the Redeemer for one's personal life *is* the basic requirement for those who desire to know God; but it is very possible to be "saved" and still miss God's purpose and plan for your life.

Let me illustrate. A father on his way home from work

decided to take his little son downtown for a treat at the ice-cream parlor. When he got home, he found his son in the backyard playing in the mud. The father didn't change his mind about the ice-cream parlor; he brought the little boy inside, gave him a bath, put clean clothes on him, and said, "Son, now we're going to the ice-cream parlor for a treat."

The little boy, being a true fundamentalist, said, "Daddy, I don't want to go. I want to stay here by the bathtub and tell everybody how dirty I was and how good you've been to me."

"But you don't understand *why* I cleaned you up," the father said; "I want you to go with me."

In II Tim. 1:9 we read: "Who hath saved us, and called us with an holy calling, not according to our works, but according to his own purpose and grace . . ." Jesus found us in the mud, cleaned us, and redeemed us from sin by His death on the cross in order that we *could* live for Him. Yet many a Christian gives thanks to God for the salvation of his soul but continues living his life in the same old way. Such Christians follow their own desires and ideas, their own guidance and initiative.

God's purpose, simply stated, was to save us *from* sin *unto* His eternal purpose. We literally owe Him our lives and one day will be held accountable for what we've done with every hour, every dime, every action, every word, every thought. If the criterion for hitting the mark is that we live our lives so totally yielded to God that His will becomes our guide, that every moment of our lives is lived in perfect accord with His plan and purpose for us, then some who are "saved" by faith in Jesus Christ have missed the mark so far it is pathetic.

How does God deal with His children when they deliberately go their own way? Does He deal with them at all, or are we free to choose our own way of life once we've entered the door of a salvation experience? Salvation is a free gift, isn't it, so why would there be any strings attached?

We are living in times of great permissiveness in child-rearing, in school discipline (or lack of it), and in rebellion against all kinds of authority whether it be parental, police, or papal. The courts where the "rights" of criminals are often considered before the rights of the innocent victims of crime just add to this national attitude. Even in our churches we are being taught situation ethics where morality is a flexible thing, not conforming to any set standard (such as that determined by the Bible). Perhaps it is time to have a lesson in justice from God who *is* justice.

In the second chapter of Jeremiah we find the prophet sent by God to warn His people who had willfully missed the mark by straying away. At one time they had walked with God. He had brought them out of Egypt and saved them from bondage. They had known His commandments and He had made a covenant with them, to bless them and make them a blessing to others. But they had persisted in going their own way. Through the words of the prophet, God reminds His people that once they loved Him, and He had protected them from evil. But then He asks: "What iniquity have your fathers found in me, that they are gone far from me, and have walked after vanity, and are become vain? Neither said they, Where is the Lord . . . ?" (Jer. 2:5–6).

There are Christians today in the same condition. God saved them from bondage, led them out of their personal Egypt, but now they go their own way; they are unaware of the absence or the presence of the Lord, for they have *forgotten* Him.

I believe there are churches today that have become such

organized marvels of religious activity, so propped up by human programs and initiative that they wouldn't miss God for a moment if He *did* die. Who needs God? They are running a business and therefore are not dependent on the supernatural manifestations of God. Like the children of Judah, no one among them is asking, "Where is the Lord?"

God describes what His people have done: "For my people have committed two evils; they have forsaken me, the fountain of living waters, and hewed them out cisterns, broken cisterns, that can hold no water" (Jer. 2:13). There is a fundamental difference between a fresh flowing well and a cistern. A cistern is hewed out of solid stone or made from concrete. Its purpose is simply to hold water that has been poured into it—water, yes, but stale and warm. In contrast, when a well is dug, it is lined with rocks, and water flows into it. At first a well doesn't give much water, and that's why we're told to keep pumping a new well dry. The more we pump, the more the water flows in, because the veins begin to clear. We've tapped an underground stream that is ever fresh and never runs dry.

The Christian who has *forsaken* the Well of Living Water has missed the mark. He's hewed out for himself instead a container for storing stale religious activity and doctrines. Instead of being a daily walk with a living Jesus, his Christianity becomes a "canned affair." Have you ever heard a sermon from a cistern? Unfortunately, there are some in almost every pastor's notebook. And the idea of a preacher reaching into his "barrel" (cistern) to find the message of the morning is more frightening than funny.

The people of Judah turned their backs on God while He was leading them in the way. This is serious business, and some of us are guilty of it today. Now what are the consequences? Some who are rebelling against God expect Him to come after them to coax and coerce, but look at Jer. 2:19: "Thine own wickedness shall correct thee, and thy backslidings shall reprove thee; know therefore and see that it is an evil thing and bitter, that thou hast forsaken the Lord, thy God, and that my fear is not in thee, saith the Lord God of hosts." When you insist on your own way, God's *cure* may be an overabundant supply of what you're asking for, until you wish you never had it.

I remember a young lady in Bible college who said, "Oh God, I must have that young man, I must." God's guidance was negative, but she kept insisting, until the restraint was lifted and God allowed them to get married. About a year and a half later, while she was still in Bible college, her husband developed a severe drinking problem. The principle of Jer. 2:19 was brought into effect as she had to help him up the stairs nearly every night.

If you insist on your own way—you're going to get it!

Later in the same chapter of Jeremiah we find another picture of the consequences of our rebellion: "A wild ass used to the wilderness, that snuffeth up the wind at her pleasure; in her occasion who can turn her away?" (Jer. 2:24). The prophet pictures human nature as a wild ass—a young donkey, self-willed and stubborn, seeking her own satisfaction and pleasure.

Have you ever been in that condition? Your course set, unyielding to reason or persuasion saying, "This is what *I'm* going to do and I could care less how it affects the will of God or anybody else"?

The last part of the verse says, "All they that seek her will not weary themselves; in her month they shall find her." What is God saying? He's saying that while we're still running, He won't send anybody to run after us. He knows that the rebellion we carry inside will bear fruit; we'll be pregnant with the consequences. In due time, while we're in labor with our full-term troubles, He'll find us and speak to us again. Hopefully, we'll be ready to listen, and open to guidance. The children of Judah were not. In Jer. 2:30 God cries through His prophet: "In vain have I smitten your children; they received no correction: your own sword hath devoured your prophets, like a destroying lion."

I know there are some people who wish that verse wasn't in the Bible. "God would never do a thing like that," they say. But God will do what He says He'll do in order to get us to listen. This we ought to realize and not deceive ourselves or blame all our misfortune on bad luck, the devil, or the national economy. Maybe God is talking to us.

But what did the children of Judah do? Their reaction is recorded in Jer. 2:31: "Why do my people say, we are lords; we will come no more unto thee?" These are God's own people speaking; they say, "We have dominion over ourselves; we'll never submit to You or Your demands on our lives. We enjoy our illegal liberty."

They're like a teenager who thought his parents were too strict. Finally reaching the omniscient age of eighteen (or maybe today it's thirteen), he kicks off all the traces and says to his father: "I'll never come under your roof again; I'm my own boss now." What can Dad say? He knows what must happen, and he'll be around to help pick up the pieces, but his father-heart wishes that he could prevent his son from hurting himself.

The children of Judah did not really believe that calamity would fall on them. They said confidently, "Because I am innocent, surely His anger shall turn from me." They were wrong. In Jer. 2:37 the prophet said, "Yea, thou shalt go forth from him, and thine hands upon thine head: for the Lord hath rejected thy confidences, and thou shalt not prosper in them." And it literally came to pass. With their hands upon their heads they were led in captivity to Babylon. They wanted to enjoy their freedom—but became slaves instead.

Yet, even then, God continued to plead with them through His prophet. In Jer. 3:4 He said, "Wilt thou not from this time cry unto me, *My Father, thou art the guide of my youth?*" What were all the teachings and dealings designed to do in their lives? God wanted them to *want* Him. "My Father, will you guide me even from my youth?"

Guidance is something we must embrace, ask for, and desire. Why are most people afraid of submitting to God's guidance?

Imagine your sixteen-year-old son. He's been getting a little wild lately, wanting some wheels, more liberty, more money. Then one day he says, "Dad, may I talk to you?"

"Sure!" You've been wanting to have a few words with him yourself.

Now he says, "Dad, I've been thinking a lot lately. You know I used to think I knew everything about life and what I was gonna do, but I'm beginning to realize that I'm still just a kid. You've been around a lot longer than me, Dad, and I'm beginning to understand that you really want what's best for me. Dad, from now on I want you to guide and direct me and show me the right way to go. Whatever you say, Dad, I'll try to obey."

Now would you say to your son, "I want you to go to your room and be restricted for six months?" Some people think that if they ever really submitted to God He would ask them to do something they can't or don't want to do. But God never demands the unjust or the impossible. He wants your submission, and in response He will tenderly guide you.

Have you ever gone your own way—and been sorry you

did? Have you ever been glad you went God's way, even if
you didn't like it at first?

That's the way it works!

There's a song we often sing in church; most of us think
of it as an appeal to the unsaved, but it's really a song of
submission—the consecration of a son to his father:

> I've wandered far away from God,
> Now I'm coming home.
> The paths of sin too long I've trod,
> Lord, I'm coming home.

Chorus:

> Coming home, coming home,
> Never more to roam,
> Open wide thine arms of love,
> Lord, I'm coming home.

To wander doesn't mean you aren't a son; it does mean
that in your rebellion and self-will you haven't submitted to
the counsel of your Father.

We know the rebellion of our human hearts. We want to
hit the mark, but when God begins to lead us we find it difficult to follow. If we're young, we say, "But, I want to live
my own life." If we're married, in business, or caught in pe-
culiar circumstances, we say, "But God, You just don't understand. In some parts of my life I've got to have my own
way; Your way is just too narrow, too strict and religious."

God *does* understand. He knows the beginning *and* the
end. He loves us with an eternal love and is working in our
lives to bring us to the place where He can daily lead us—in
finances, in our relationships with others, in physical needs,
in our spiritual walk.

As you submit to guidance, you'll find God taking the *initiative* in your life, adjusting and rearranging where you've been off the track. If you say, "Yes, Lord," to Him, you'll find Him leading you in a new way. And, by the way, you'll never find His demands greater than what you can produce. Phil. 2:13 promises us: "For it is God who worketh in you both to will and to do of his good pleasure." Later in the same letter Paul writes: "I am ready for anything through the strength of the one who lives within me" (Phil. 4:13 Phillips).

God is not guilty of being willing to guide some and not others. We shut ourselves off from genuine guidance by following our own desires and coating them with a veneer of pretended obedience. Human desires are masked as guidance in order to make rebellion palatable to ourselves and others. The result is self-deception and a rejection of true guidance. The monumental illustration of this is Saul, the king of Israel, who in self-will refused to obey, causing Samuel to declare: "For rebellion is as the sin of witchcraft, and stubbornness is as idolatry and teraphim (good luck images). Because you have rejected the word of the Lord, He also has rejected you from being king" (I Sam. 15:23, *Amplified Bible*).

Divine guidance is for all of God's children who *ask* to be guided, *submit* to Him who is the Guide, and *refuse* to follow their own human desires.

CHAPTER

3

LUCK ... OR HAPPENSTANCE?

When we, like errant sons and daughters, return to our Father and say, "Dad, I want you to be the guide of my youth," something begins to happen. God begins to guide our lives in a new way. We misunderstand greatly, however, if we believe this is always going to happen in some spectacular way.

When we talk about divine guidance, most people think in terms of dreams, visions, prophecies, angels, and voices. These all have a place in divine guidance. But *most* guidance occurs when we're not even conscious of it. God knows the beginning and the end. He arranges circumstances. Sometimes we are required to take another look at where we've been in order to realize that God has even been guiding us at all.

When we take a closer look at the cases of obvious guidance in the Bible—and in our own lives—we may discover that direct interference from God is usually for the purpose of adjusting or correcting the way of His children, much as a space scientist would make an inflight course correction on a rocket speeding toward the moon. This may come as a blow to our spiritual pride, for we would like to say: "I am becoming spiritual; God led me this evening. He let me have a flat tire on the way to the airport. I missed my flight and the plane crashed on takeoff killing everyone on board." This is not to say God does not sometimes work sensationally, but usually God's guidance is so natural that the Spirit-led Christian won't even be aware of it.

God's providence works on a narrow, dangerous margin. This, I believe, is a fundamental principle in divine guidance. God is required to interfere directly in our lives to prevent us from messing up the plan He has for us. An accident, a phone-call, a chance meeting, a perfectly timed letter, causes us to look back and say, "Praise the Lord! He knew the beginning and the end. He led me even when I didn't know it."

This form of guidance is what we'll term unconscious guidance, and it begins when we meet several conditions— the first being that we must place ourselves in a childlike relationship to God and submit to His will for our life. Often, in the eternal council of God, it has operated before we ever made this discovery.

This initial commitment to God is something like getting on a train. Once you're on board you don't worry about the intersections, the red and green lights. They are the engineer's job. *Your* responsibility is to get on the right train.

Once I was having lunch in a Philadelphia restaurant and got into a conversation with a waitress who was not a believer in Jesus Christ. She said, "Well, I feel like I'm sincere and that's what counts, isn't it? As long as you're sincere it doesn't really matter what you believe. We're all going to the same place in the end."

I thought, *Dear Lord, what am I going to say to this lady?* Then I remembered about the train. "What if you want to go to Miami," I said, "and you get on a train bound for New

York City? You sit there and say, 'I believe. I believe I'm going to Miami.' And you're very sincere about it. Now when that train pulls into Grand Central Station, where do you think you'll be, in New York, or Miami?"

"Oh," she said, "I understand." I hope she did because *sincerity is not guidance.*

How then does this "unconscious" form of guidance work? Let's look at a couple of examples in the Bible. The first one is in the Book of Ruth.

Naomi was a widow and she was returning to her native Israel. Her daughter-in-law, Ruth, was a gentile. Naomi said, "Ruth, you must stay here in your own land, find yourself a husband and live happily with him." But Ruth refused to stay. She clung to Naomi and said, "Intreat me not to leave thee, or to return from following after thee: for whither thou goest, I will go; and where thou lodgest, I will lodge: thy people shall be my people, and thy God my God" (Ruth 1:16). Ruth committed herself to Naomi and to God. She wanted to serve her and her God forever, even until death. She said, "Where thou diest, will I die, and there will I be buried: the Lord do so to me, and more also, if ought but death part thee and me" (Ruth 1:17).

Now this is unreserved commitment to God, a presupposition for guidance, and the lack of it is the cause of many problems in divine guidance.

God's response to that *kind* of commitment is found in Ruth 2:12: "The Lord recompense thy work, and a full reward be given thee of the Lord God of Israel, under whose wings thou art come to trust." Ruth had put herself into God's hands and He promised to keep her.

So Naomi and Ruth went back to Bethlehem, Naomi's hometown. But outwardly they did not see the immediate fulfillment of God's promised blessing. Things were rough for them. They were poor, and one day the poverty caused Ruth to go out and find some grain to make their bread. This was during the barley harvest, and the poor were allowed to come into the fields after the reapers had gathered the grain and glean what the reapers had overlooked. Things were so bad she had to live as a scavenger. There was still no outward evidence of God's guidance and concern.

Now notice an interesting verse: "And she went, and came, and gleaned in the field after the reapers: and her *hap* was to light on a part of the field belonging unto Boaz, who was of the kindred of Elimelech" (Ruth 2:3). Elimelech was Naomi's husband who had died.

How did Ruth get her guidance so that she *just happened* to glean in Boaz's field? Did she say, "Oh, God, speak to me in a vision and tell me what field to glean in?" No, Ruth was simply doing her duty, working her way patiently between the rows, picking up the few grains she could find, and she just happened to wind up in Boaz's field.

The world calls it *luck*. The Christian calls it *providence!* But as Ruth was concentrating on doing her duty, her *hap* happened. She was in the right field at the right time doing the right thing to meet the right man. And so, because of her unreserved commitment to God and her willingness to do menial tasks even when she did not see God's providence at work, He arranged the circumstances. Ruth married Boaz, and they had a son who became David's grandfather. Ruth is one of the few gentiles in the lineage of Jesus Christ and it is thrilling to think of how she just *happened* to be in that position.

How many times we just *happen* to be in the right place at the right time!

An evangelist tells the story of driving across Florida with his family. When his wife said, "Let's stop in this town and get some orange juice for the children," he agreed and they just *happened* to turn off at a certain exit, drove down a block or two, and *happened* to pull up in front of a certain fruit-stand. Before he had time to get out of the car a lady came running across the street.

"Are you a minister?" she asked breathlessly.

"Yes," he replied.

"Praise the Lord!" she exclaimed. "This morning I prayed that God would send a minister who would lay hands on me and pray for my healing. God said you'd be driving a station wagon and be pulling a trailer." She looked at the evangelist's brown station wagon and trailer and asked, "What took you so long?"

The evangelist and his wife didn't know anything about God's plan for them that afternoon. They hadn't heard a voice say, "Turn off at this exit and drive two blocks to the fruit-stand where there is a lady I want you to pray for." But they *had* committed that day to God and prayed before leaving that His will and plan for that day would come to pass. When we do this, we begin to find ourselves in the right places at the right time for God's providence to work in our behalf. It is adventuresome!

Let's look at some other conditions for perfect "unconscious" guidance. The story of Abraham's servant, who is sent to find a wife for Isaac, is a classic example of guidance. "And the man bowed down his head, and worshipped the Lord. And he said, Blessed be the Lord God of my master Abraham, who hath not left destitute my master of his mercy and his truth: *I being in the way, the Lord led me* to the house of my master's brethren" (Gen. 24:26–27).

Now if we look at the entire story in this chapter, we find at least *three* specific presuppositions for this kind of perfect unconscious guidance.

In verses 3–4 Abraham had said to his oldest and most trusted servant: "And I will make thee swear by the Lord, the God of heaven, and the God of earth, that thou shalt not take a wife unto my son of the daughters of the Canaanites, among whom I dwell: But thou shalt go unto my country, and to my kindred, and take a wife unto my son Isaac."

The *first* premise: the servant was made to promise to maintain a separation from the world. Abraham wanted Isaac to be holy and undefiled in the presence of the Lord. This is the first condition in qualifying for God's "unconscious guidance" in our lives.

Now look at verse 7: "The Lord God of heaven, who took me from my father's house, and from the land of my kindred, and who spoke unto me, and who swore unto me, saying, Unto thy seed will I give this land; he shall send his angel before thee, and thou shalt take a wife unto my son from there."

The *second* premise: they believed the word of God. Abraham said, "Listen, God promised to find us a wife and we believe it." This trust was a fundamental aspect of his relationship with God, and a second vital condition in our being open to God's guidance.

Now look at verses 12–14: The servant obtained ten camels and started on his way saying, "O Lord, God of my master Abraham, I pray thee, send me good speed this day, and show kindness unto my master Abraham."

Third premise: The whole thing was soaked in prayer. I don't mean just prayer for specifics, I mean soaked, steeped in prayer. The servant's soul was poised toward God—a final condition we must practice in our lives if we are to be in position to appropriate God's guidance.

The servant came to the well outside the city at evening time, knowing the women would come out to draw water.

He continued talking to God in prayer: "Behold, I stand here by the well of water; and the daughters of the men of the city come out to draw water: And let it come to pass, that the damsel to whom I shall say, Let down thy pitcher, I pray thee, that I may drink; and she shall say, Drink, and I will give thy camels drink also; let her be the one whom thou hast appointed for thy servant, Isaac; and thereby shall I know that thou hast shown kindness unto my master."

What happened? Read verse 15: "And it came to pass, before he had finished speaking, that, behold, Rebekah came out . . ." Do you think God had whispered in Rebekah's ear, "Rebekah, I want you to go to the well; there's a man up there . . ."? No, Rebekah, just like Ruth, came to the well because it was time to draw water. It was her duty to be there.

Had God whispered in the servant's ear, "Go to that well; I'll send a damsel"? No, the servant went to the well because he was tired, sweaty, and thirsty after a long day's travel. He stood there, not knowing what to do next. It was in desperation that he said, "I'm going to trust you, Lord. The first damsel I speak to who volunteers to draw water for me and my camels will be the one, Lord."

And when it happened, when Rebekah gave the servant a drink from her pitcher and volunteered to draw water for his camels, the servant bowed his head and worshiped God: "Oh, Lord, I thank You. I didn't know where to find a bride for Isaac, but You led me over thousands of miles and I just happened to come to the right well at the right time to meet the right woman."

First there is a commitment which involves a separation unto God. Second, a trusting in His word, His promises. And finally, a life steeped in prayer, a soul poised toward God.

That's getting on the right train. The rest is up to the engineer and the conductor.

So far we've been dealing with unconscious, providential guidance. But if during our journey it becomes necessary to change trains, who is responsible for letting us know when to get off and which one to take next? The conductor, of course. If God the Father is the engineer, then the conductor must be the Holy Spirit.

To change trains we need special guidance. That's when the conductor comes along with a dream, a vision, a prophetic word, a miracle, or some other kind of specific direction.

So we're talking about two forms of guidance—the unconscious, providential guidance because our lives are committed to Jesus Christ, and the special guidance when God wants to move us into a new direction, a new job, a new field.

An example of this is found in Luke 2:27 and again in Luke 2:38. Simeon had received a special revelation from the Holy Spirit that he should go to the Temple. He arrived just at the time the parents of Jesus brought the child for circumcision. However, old Anna received no such special revelation. She was always going to the Temple to fast and pray, and she just "happened" to arrive at the time the Christ child appeared. But both Simeon and Anna were there by divine timing.

Perhaps you have said, "Well, if I could hear a voice I'd be at the right place at the right time, too." But look at Anna who just happened to be there. Like Ruth and Rebekah she was just doing her duty, and God blessed her in the process.

The teaching object of this is to relieve the strain of feeling that since we don't hear voices we can't be guided. God leads one by voices and another by circumstances. But He leads both to Christ. Once we've made our commitment to the Lord we can *expect* to be in the right field, by the right well, in the right temple, or on the right street at the right time.

4

KNOWING *THE WILL OF GOD!*

As Christians we too often major in minors. We pray, "Oh, Lord, help us pay the rent. Help me find a new job. I need a new car, Lord." Those should be our minor concerns.

Paul approached things differently. He had a specific request for the brand new church at Colossae: ". . . we . . . do not cease to pray for you, and to desire that ye might be *filled* with the knowledge of his *will* in all wisdom and spiritual understanding" (Col. 1:9). This is majoring in majors. The basic and underlying premise for all divine guidance is that it is possible to *know* the will of God! This should be at the top of our prayer list for ourselves and others.

God originally created man that He might have communion with him. Man was created with the ability to know God. But man's rebellion and sin (his inability to "hit the mark") broke the lines of communication. Through Christ we've been given the opportunity to restore that intimate fellowship with God, and this is the goal which we're seeking. *Learning the skill of receiving divine guidance is learning to walk in intimate fellowship with God.* The problem at the outset is that our minds and our intellects are quite out of tune with God and blinded by the sin within and around us.

At night I often lay my hands on my children and pray, "Oh, God, give them a capacity to know You." If they come to know God, everything else in their lives will fall into place. Jesus said it too: "Seek ye first the kingdom of God, and his righteousness; and all these things shall be added unto you" (Matt. 6:33).

Paul had observed what happened in a man's life when he came to know the will of God. In his letter to the Colossians he lists seven expected results: "That ye might *walk worthy* of the Lord *unto all pleasing,* being *fruitful* in every good work, and *increasing in the knowledge* of God; *Strengthened* with all might, according to his glorious power, unto all *patience and long-suffering with joyfulness;* Giving thanks unto the Father, who hath made us *fit to be partakers* of the inheritance of the saints in light" (Col. 1:10–12). In order to *walk worthy* of the Lord we must know what He wants from us. Jesus walked *unto all pleasing;* He was a Father-pleaser.

God once impressed on me the need to focus in on a single goal for my life. One by one my prayer requests were reduced to one specific prayer: "Father, I want to be a son who can please You." I began to realize God wanted me to major in majors.

Most men are *self-pleasers.* Others are *man-pleasers.* But until men reach the stage of wanting to be *God-pleasers* they will never be able to fully understand the will of the Father for their lives. And it is only by doing the will of God that our lives become fruitful. Perhaps you've met people who've been "saved" for years, yet never led another person to Christ. They complain, "What's the matter with me? Maybe I should read a book on how to win souls and influence people!" They don't need to read a book; they need to be in the will of God.

Can you imagine an apple tree crying out, "Oh, Lord, please bring forth apples from my life"? An apple tree doesn't have to pray to bear apples. It *has* to bring forth the life that is in it; this is the act for which it was created, and it shouldn't have to strain to produce. Fruit should come naturally. When we are in the will of God, *knowing* the will of God for our lives, we'll bring forth fruit, the kind of fruit God wants each of us to bear.

Knowing the will of God we *increase in the knowledge* of God and we're *strengthened* with all might according to His glorious power. That's strength!

Christians often complain of their weakness, rather than glory in their available strength. "It takes all the power I have just to stay right with God," they say. "Please pray for me. I need more joy, more victory in my life." Sure, I could pray, but ten minutes later they'd feel down again. If they would seek to know God's will for their lives and *stay* in that will, they'd be strengthened with all might according to His glorious power unto all *patience* and *long-suffering* with *joyfulness*.

When you *know* you're in the will of God you can stand almost any hardship. The trouble arises when we're not sure a particular thing is God's will for us. Then there is confusion inside, and patience goes out the door. The Greek word for patience is *hupomone* and freely translated it means to remain standing after everyone else has collapsed. We've all known people who have gone through great trials and hardships yet have exhibited great joy, vitality, and victory through it all. They can do it because somehow they've come to know that it was God's will for them, and they thank Him for it, joyfully.

When you *know* the will of God you can give *thanks* to the Father in all circumstances. The Bible tells us to give thanks *in everything*, and that means while you're going through hardship—not just after it's over. I've learned to practice that, giving thanks at times when the circumstances were anything but good. I say, "Father, I thank You for this. I thank You for Your will, I thank You for *all* things, in Christ Jesus, because You do not permit accidents to come into my life."

I don't believe in accidents; I cannot believe in luck. Furthermore, the devil cannot pull a fast one while God isn't looking. If God has a hand in everything that happens to me, I'm going to thank Him for it, even if it doesn't make much sense to me at the moment. I have learned that God knows more about it than I do.

Paul speaks of "giving thanks unto the Father Who hath . . . made us *fit* [the original meaning is *capable*] to be partakers of the inheritance of the saints in light; Who hath delivered us from the power of darkness, and hath translated us into the kingdom of his dear Son" (Col. 1:12–13 various trans.). Paul isn't saying *maybe!* He says God has already made us capable, in Jesus Christ, to be partakers of our inheritance. This isn't a promise about life after death. It is valid now.

How much of God's will are we capable of knowing and doing? Surely we frail and fallible human beings can only hope to begin to live up to just a small part of God's perfect plan for our lives.

But look at what Paul writes in Col. 4:12: "Epaphras, who is one of you, a servant of Christ, saluteth you, always labouring fervently for you in prayers, that ye may stand *perfect* and *complete* in *all* the will of God." Paul prayed that we should know and do all of God's will for our life.

Each of us should earnestly ask: "Father, what do You want from my life? What do You want for me and my family? What do You want for my finances, my capabilities, and my talents? All that I have and all that I am? I want to know and to do all of the will which You have for me."

It is possible for us to *know* and *do* all the will of God for our lives. But how do we go about it? What's the next step?

The formula is found in Rom. 12:1–2: "I beseech you therefore, brethren, by the mercies of God, that ye present your bodies a living sacrifice, holy, acceptable unto God, which is your reasonable service. And be not conformed to this world: but be ye transformed by the renewing of your mind, that ye may prove what is that good, and acceptable, and *perfect, will of God.*"

Paul says that we should be *transformed* by the renewing of our mind. The word "transformed" is the same word used to describe what happened to Jesus on the Mount of Transfiguration. The disciples saw Jesus with Moses and Elijah. As He was transfigured, His whole countenance was changed by the Glory of God. That's what Paul wants for us, that our minds be "transfigured" by the Glory of God. We need to learn to think differently from how we ever thought before. The *ability* to *know* the will of God requires a changing, a renewing of our minds.

J. B. Phillips translates this passage this way: "With eyes wide open to the mercies of God, I beg you, my brothers, as an act of intelligent worship, to give him your bodies, as a living sacrifice, consecrated to him and acceptable by him. Don't let the world around you squeeze you into its own mold, but *let God remold* your minds from within, so that you may prove in practice that the plan of God for you is good, meets all his demands and moves toward the goal of true maturity."

When God remolds our minds we'll think differently.

We'll see things in a different light. We won't interpret things the way we used to. There'll be a difference in our understanding.

Imagine a little boy looking through a knothole in the fence at a parade going by on the street. He can see just a little bit of the parade at a time. If he sees a clown he's full of joy. If he sees a lion he's afraid. If there is a space between the band and the acrobats he may even think the parade is over. And if someone stands in front of the knothole he sees nothing. It is a very frustrating experience since he evaluates the parade only on the basis of what he sees (or can't see) at that moment.

Then there's a voice calling his name. His older brother has climbed up on top of the roof and says, "Come on up. You can see much better from here!"

The little boy scampers up on the rooftop and from there he can see the whole length of the street below. He can see the beginning of the parade, the middle of it, and the end. It's wonderful. He's seeing things in a new perspective and it isn't the way it looked through a knothole in the fence at all.

When we look at life through a knothole we can see only what's right before our eyes, viewing and evaluating circumstances on the basis of the here and now. I see only that my wife is sick, my bankbook is empty, my brother in Vietnam is wounded. This is the short look at life. God can see that too, but ever so much more. When we get our eye from the knothole and take the place where we rightfully belong, we will see things from a new perspective too. This is looking at circumstances as God looks—taking the long look.

In Eph. 2:6 Paul described where we belong: "And [He] hath raised us up together, and made us sit together in heavenly places in Christ Jesus."

A sign on a man's desk said, "Keep looking down." We see plenty of signs saying, "Keep looking up," but never one like that. When asked what the sign meant, the man said, "I used to be on earth, looking up. Now I am seated with Christ in heavenly places and I'm looking down! The view from up there is quite different."

I found myself praying, "Father, help me to see things and people as You see them."

It can be frightening at times. We see a man and draw our own conclusions: "That old drunken bum!"

And the Lord says, "Don't you talk like that. That's one of my jewels. I just haven't polished him yet."

"But Lord, that doesn't look like a jewel to me!" The Lord says, "You wait till I'm done with him. I'm going to use you to polish him!"

God's viewpoint isn't like ours. In Isa. 55:8–9 we read: "For my thoughts are not your thoughts, neither are your ways my ways, saith the Lord. For as the heavens are higher than the earth, so are my ways higher than your ways and my thoughts than your thoughts."

Last year a housewife in Wisconsin gave her heart to Christ and accepted Him as her Savior. That night she read in her Bible, "Believe on the Lord Jesus Christ, and thou shalt be saved, and thy house" (Acts 16:31). She dropped to her knees and claimed the latter part of this verse as a promise that the Lord would save her husband. She was sure she knew just how it would happen. Her husband would come along with her to church. He would go forward and accept the Lord.

But her husband happened to hear her while she prayed. He became furious. "Shut up, woman! Don't try any of that religious stuff on me!"

So she came back to church the next night and com-

plained: "I don't understand it. Ever since I started praying for my husband he's gotten worse."

My response: "Praise the Lord! God's ways are *not* like your ways. The man who is angry is closer to God than the man who is indifferent. Rev. 3:15–16 reads: 'I would that thou wert cold or hot . . . because thou art lukewarm . . . I will spue thee out of my mouth.'" Because she had claimed her promise, her husband was already closer than he was before.

When a man gets angry in a meeting where I am teaching and stomps out muttering, "That stupid guy and his teachings!" I say, "Bless him, Lord." I know, at least, that an angry man isn't lukewarm.

When you begin to pray for someone to accept Christ you have to realize that God will do it *His* way. Whether he finds Christ in church, in his own living room, or while he's out fishing is none of your business!

Unless we experience the transformation of our thinking, we can never understand the full will of God. As men we are always trying to read our will into it. Often we try to tell God how to work.

God will not permit Himself to be put into a box where we can anticipate His every move. He is sovereign and does what He wants to do. He *is* the King of the Earth, and not subject to our earthly or logical formulas. He refuses to permit us to anticipate Him or to "help Him" figure out how to do things.

In Rom. 12:2 Paul gives us the practical outline for mind renewal. First, he says, "Don't." *Don't* let the world squeeze you into its mold. Don't be conformed to this age. That means we must refuse to permit our thinking to follow the pattern of this world.

We are living in the days of mass media, and it's hard to

be the only family on the block without a tiger in the tank of your car. New fads are sweeping our nation in a matter of weeks. Short hair, long hair, short skirts, long skirts. Shaving lotions, breakfast cereals, Slinkys, Hula-Hoops, Yo-Yos, Clackers. What's happening? It is my personal opinion that this is how the world is being brainwashed in preparation for national manipulation and Madison Avenue psychosis. Refuse to let your mind be captivated, conformed, squeezed into the mold of this world!

Now a positive step: ". . . let your mind be renewed, let God remold your mind from within . . ." *Invite* the changing of your mind. *Embrace* the transforming work of the Holy Spirit. *Say* to God: "Here's my mind, Lord, my old habit thoughts; take them and give me a new mind; let that mind which was in Christ be in me."

That's a scriptural prayer. In Phil. 2:5 Paul says, "Let this mind be in you, which was also in Christ Jesus."

As we pray earnestly, God begins to remold our minds. He enables us to think the thoughts of Christ. We begin to see things as God sees them.

In Rom. 12:1 Paul tells us how to do it. By deliberately giving ourselves, our bodies, a living sacrifice to God, we open the door for God's transforming power to sweep through our entire being.

We know that the Holy Spirit is a gentleman. He never forces His entry into our lives. He must be invited. The transforming of our beings into the perfect image of God doesn't happen automatically. Some Christians appear to think that once they've invited Jesus Christ at the time of salvation, He takes care of all the rest. But the *initiative* remains ours. If not, it would not have been necessary for Paul to urge the Roman Christians to give themselves, their bodies, as an act of *intelligent* worship (that is, as a deliberate, well-thought-out act of commitment, not an emotional, frenzied self-sacrifice), a *living* sacrifice. We are often far more eager to die for Jesus Christ than to live for Him. Be a living sacrifice, He says, daily dying to your selfish motives and desires. God wants a practical, deliberate, daily surrender of our lives, our bodies, so that He may use us. We must pray, "Here I am, Lord. All of me. Remake me, use me this day, Lord."

When God begins to remold our minds from within, we may find ourselves at odds with the world in a new way. Jesus said: "Ye are they which justify yourselves before men; but God knoweth your hearts: for that which is highly esteemed among men is *abomination* in the sight of God" (Luke 16:15). This means that sometimes you're going to stand quite alone against something everybody else may think of highly.

There is a new principle here: What man acclaims as *the answer* is often the very *opposite* of what God wants to do. Man says: "What we need is a brand new, three-million-dollar sanctuary with padded pews. *Then* the people will come to church!"

Is that God's solution?

There were two or three million Jews who all wanted to go back to Egypt when they came to the edge of the Red Sea. But Moses said: "Oh, no you don't, because God says we're going *this* way!" Had they called a church business meeting and taken a vote, the count would have been two million to one. But the Israelites were looking through a knothole, while Moses was up on top of the house. With an expanded vision and a transformed mind Moses could see the entire parade route across the Red Sea, beyond the wilderness and into the Promised Land. The democratic process is not always the best way, especially when folks don't have the "mind of Christ" and are looking through knot-holes when they should be seeking a higher view.

The change that takes place when you allow God to renew your mind brings you into a new and glorious liberty where you will be able to walk with Jesus and find yourself able to make decisions in the light of God's eternal purpose. You begin to know what it is to stand firm and not be influenced by every new doctrine, idea, or fad (cf. Eph. 4:14). You are free to receive guidance from God.

CHAPTER

5

OUTSIDE GOD'S WILL

How do we know whether we're in the will of God or out of it?

We've taken our first steps toward learning to recognize the guiding hand of God in our personal lives: we've seen and confessed our own rebellion and made a deliberate commitment of our lives to God in Christ. We've taken Paul's advice in Rom. 12:1–2 and given our physical bodies, a living sacrifice to God. We recognize that one of the results of that move is a gradual change in our very thinking process as God begins to remold our minds from within. So now, with our new perspective, we stop and take another look at ourselves and our surroundings.

In order to find out *where* we are in the will of God, it is sometimes helpful to ask ourselves *how* we are. In Deut. 28:65–67 we find a list of symptoms. Now symptoms is a good word. We all know what it means in medical terms. When we have a persistent pain we call it a symptom. It tells us that something is wrong. We recognize the symptom as a signal for us to do something about it. Maybe we have a broken leg, an infected appendix, or an abscessed tooth.

A symptom calls for a diagnosis and then for action. Some

people live with symptoms and do nothing about them. They get so used to an aching tooth or a sore back that they think it's normal to feel that way.

There are many Christians who live with the symptoms of being out of God's will and think that's normal. The writer of Deuteronomy says: ". . . you shall find *no ease* and there shall be *no rest* for the sole of your foot; but the Lord will give you there a *trembling heart, failing of eyes* (from disappointment of hope), *fainting of mind* and *languishing of spirit.* Your life shall *hang in doubt* before you; day and night you shall be *worried,* and have *no assurance* of your life. In the morning you shall say, Would it were evening! and at evening you shall say, Would it were morning! because of the *anxiety* and *dread* of your [mind and] heart, and the sights which you shall *see* with your [own] eyes" (Deut. 28:65–67 *Amplified Bible*).

Look at the symptoms within you and around you. Uneasiness! Have you ever noticed our teenagers? They can't stand it without noise—transistor radios, television, and phonograph blaring while they do their homework. You try to turn off the noisemakers and they say, "Please, Dad, I can't concentrate when it's quiet!"

Restlessness! A fainting or sorrowing of mind! Depression! Do you feel it? What do you do about it? Take anti-depressant pills, tranquilizers, or pray for God to take away your worries?

Uncertainty. Fearfulness. Anxiety. Every time you hear the fire engine or the police siren do you have a queasy feeling in your stomach, fearing it's your house, your kids? What if a burglar comes tonight? What if a famine strikes? What if we have an all-out war or a bad flu epidemic? I hear Christians talk of worry, and I cringe. They are exhibiting symptoms of being out of the center of God's will.

A retired medical missionary lives by herself in a little cottage right in the middle of a ghetto in a Florida town. There have been some lootings, burnings, and demonstrations around her. Every time it happens, her friends ask, "Aren't you afraid of being alone at night? Maybe you ought to get a big watchdog!"

The lady always smiles and shakes her head. "There is no safer place in the whole world than in the center of God's will. He placed me here, and He is my mighty fortress."

All around us we see men's hearts failing them for fear, lack of assurance, and discontent. What are the final symptoms? The Bible tells us: "And the Lord shall bring you into Egypt again with ships, by the way about which I said to you, You shall never see it again; and there you shall be sold to your enemies for bondmen and bondwomen, and no man shall buy you" (Deut. 28:68 *Amplified Bible*). In other words, if we allow these symptoms to persist they will lead us into final spiritual bondage.

Where do the symptoms come from?

Most of us blame them on circumstances. We say, "I lie awake worrying at night because I lost my job. If I could only get another job I wouldn't worry." Now seen from a human point of view that is a perfectly reasonable explanation for our anxiety and sleeplessness. So we get a few sleeping tablets to carry us over the rough spot. If we're Christian we might call the prayer-band in our church and have them pray for a new job. We might even talk to the minister and have him pray for our "nerves." However, verse 65 in the chapter we just read says: ". . . the *Lord* shall give thee there a trembling heart . . ."

From our new perspective we should take another look at our unemployment. "Did *You* allow that to happen, Lord? Did You want me to discover my own anxiety and look for a deeper cause—knowing this was far more important than keeping my job?"

Since God began to bring about a change in my way of thinking I don't look at the calamities in my life the way I used to. I'm beginning to realize they are there to expose symptoms: pride, rebellion, fear, insecurity, lack of assurance. We need these things to crowd us into God. I wish we were all so obedient that such hardships wouldn't be necessary, but we're not. And so I've started to thank God when He allows troubles to come into my life.

If God didn't have use for the devil, He would have bound him and cast him into the pit thousands of years ago. Why, then, does God permit him to exist? Simply because Satan is the one who creates the needs that drive us to Jesus. When things are fine and in a rut, who needs Jesus? But suddenly the children are sick, the transmission fails on our car, and we're back on our knees, praying.

We make a mistake when we call our symptoms "needs" and simply pray that God remove them. Like the pain from a ruptured appendix or the dizziness from a brain tumor, symptoms are there for a reason. God means for us to let Him expose the deeper cause and heal us. Relief from pain could be the most tragic thing that ever happened, unless the cause was removed.

Most of us are escape artists. We'll use any excuse to keep from facing up to our own failings. Modern psychology has provided us several new escape mechanisms. Most of us have been influenced by some aspects of the Freudian theories about our psychological problems.

Freud describes our ego (self) as being trapped somewhere between the id (our natural appetites and desires) and the superego (our conscience). Freud says the id is an expression of what we *want* to do, and these wants are regulated by the superego which reminds us what we've been taught that we ought or ought not to do. Problems arise when the conflicts between our wants and cannots become too strong. In psychological circles these conflicts are known as "frustrations." In Freudian thinking, the solution lies in removing the restrictions so that the ego (self) won't become warped by guilt complexes. This is called "adjusting."

In the Navy I had a shipmate who was about to crack up. As the ship's medic I took him to the base psychiatrist in Japan. He spent about forty-five minutes in the doctor's office. When he came out he said, "Bob, do you know what the doctor told me? He said for me to go ashore, get me the best prostitute in Japan, get cockeyed drunk, and I'd be all right in the morning."

My friend took the doctor's advice. Did his guilt feelings increase or decrease?

Two months later he had a total breakdown on board ship. With a loaded gun he retreated to a forward hold and had to be removed by force and committed to a mental institution. He didn't need to adjust his superego disciplines to the animal drives of his id. Rather, he needed his id transformed by the power of God. Sad to say, this is the one thing the psychiatrist deemed impossible. As a Freudian theorist, he read the symptom as the cause and prescribed "adjustment" as the cure, when what my shipmate really needed was a good old-fashioned dose of repentance.

Magazines and books on child-rearing and education often teach that young people must be allowed freedom to express themselves, or their personalities will be warped. Today we are reaping the consequences of such teachings in an increased lawlessness, lack of respect for property, authority, and individuals. The so-called new morality teaches we are not responsible for what we do—if we have the desire to do it. It must be legal, or God wouldn't have given us the desire in the first place, the new school teaches.

Our mental hospitals and psychiatric clinics are full of miserable people who've been told that their problems arise from excessive guilt feelings imposed on them by the narrow, puritanical teachings they received at home or in Sunday school. Millions of Americans consume tons of tranquilizers and drink gallons of alcohol to ease their symptoms while they plunge headlong into more excessive self-expression to find release from their guilt complexes.

Fortunately, the last few years have seen the beginning of a reversal in thought among leading psychiatrists. A new theory, called Reality Therapy, is gaining recognition. Christians will say that the "new theory" is as old as the Bible. It teaches that we are responsible for what we do, and that feelings of guilt are not only normal but healthy. In fact, it is abnormal not to feel guilty when we oppose and rebel against God. And the built-in pressures of guilt feelings are designed to drive us back to the source so that we can make the wrong right.

As Christians we recognize, of course, that God's grace is the answer to our guilt, and that confession will bring release and restoration. Unconfessed sin is like a festering sore. A Band-Aid or a tranquilizer will not bring healing, only a temporary hiding or escape from the symptom.

In Reality Therapy, psychiatrists recognize that wrong actions give rise to guilt feelings. For example, if I'm supposed to be at work at eight o'clock and I sleep until five minutes of eight, I get to the office at 8:15 and have bad feelings inside. I don't want to see the boss. He says, "Bob, how come you were late this morning?" I say, "Well, uh, er, there was a traffic jam." The bad feelings inside me increase. First I did something wrong, then I lied to cover it up, and before I know it I'm getting in deeper and deeper. I get a headache. I'm grumpy all day, and that night I can't go to sleep without a sleeping pill.

Now the quickest way to get rid of this thing before it builds up any worse is to swallow my pride and rectify the situation by telling the boss the truth. Granted, this will cause a new set of problems, but at least I can go to work combating them because they are founded on truth. Problems built on a lie can never be solved until the lie is corrected.

A college student was admitted to a mental hospital. All day long he sat in a corner without moving, staring vacantly ahead. The counselors tried to talk to him about his childhood, his friends in school. What had caused this terrible regression? Was it his mother? A frightening experience in school? Somewhere, surely, his tender soul had been bruised, his mind given a shock. He didn't respond.

Then they decided to try Reality Therapy. The counselor said, "All right, what are you trying to forget? What did you do wrong?" The student began to cry, and the staff psychiatrist said, "You're being too hard on him; better treat him with kid gloves."

For several days the sessions went on. The counselor urged the boy to confess what he'd done and the boy broke down and cried. Finally he came out with it: "My dad worked hard and sacrificed to put me in college," he said. "While I was there I cheated on my work, lied, and ran around with a girl when I should have been studying. At midterm I was failing, and instead of facing up to what I'd done, I went into a slump. My friends said, 'What's the matter, Norman?' I passed them off saying I just didn't feel good. They said, 'Poor Norman, do you want some help?' Day by day I got worse. I fed on their sympathy and finally I just sat there like a vegetable."

The counselor advised Norman to go back to his father and face the music. He did. The following year he went back to college, graduated, and went on to live a normal, successful life.

The Bible story about the prodigal son is a classic example of the same kind of experience. The son wasted his inheritance, and when the symptoms became bad enough, he returned to his father, confessed, asked forgiveness, and was restored.

In Psalm 32 David said: "Blessed is he whose transgression is forgiven, whose sin is covered . . . I acknowledged my sin unto thee, and mine iniquity have I not hid. I said, I will confess my transgressions unto the Lord; and thou forgavest the iniquity of my sin" (Psa. 32:1,5). What was David's sin? He had committed adultery and murder and lied about it. When the pressures became too great he confessed, acknowledged his sin to God, and received forgiveness and release. This is Reality Therapy that has run its full course.

Why do Americans consume more medicine than any other nation on earth? We are trying to escape facing ourselves.

The first escape artist was Adam. God came after Adam and said, "What have you done?" Adam said, "It was that woman you gave me; she's to blame." Then God asked Eve, and she became the second escape artist. She blamed the serpent. This escape process is often at the root of our emotional distress!

When things don't go right in our lives we blame everybody else. Maybe the Bible is wrong. Maybe the pastor who prayed for me didn't have enough faith. Maybe God isn't listening. Maybe it's an attack of Satan. Maybe it's because my mother forced me when I was a child. We blame everybody but ourselves. We're Freudian oriented, and so we fall in love with the church youth worker. She's married and the mother of two children. We say, "I can't help it; every time I see her in church I get funny feelings, and I can't help it."

You better help it! The Bible says we're responsible, and Jesus doesn't mince His words about adultery: "Anyone who *looks* at a woman and lusteth after her committeth adultery in his heart." Those words wouldn't be in the Book if God had made us incapable of disciplining our feelings.

Freudian psychology would lead us to believe that an alcoholic is sick. However, drunkenness is sin! It is a chemical escape from reality. In Alcoholics Anonymous they have a twelve-step program to sobriety. The first step is to confess you're an alcoholic. The second step is to turn to God. That's Reality Therapy. In Christian terms we call it repentance and faith.

Homosexuality is a condition that can't be helped, says our modern generation, clamoring for the "rights" of the homosexuals. But the Bible calls it sin, and says we are to refuse it and be delivered from it.

Once there was a young man leading the song-service in a large church in New York City. Suddenly he stopped and said, "People, tonight is a very crucial night for me." Everyone was very quiet watching him. He went on: "If the Lord Jesus doesn't help me tonight, I don't know where I'll ever get help. I'm a homosexual."

For years he had excused himself saying, "My mother overshadowed me. My father deserted us. It's *their* fault I'm this way." But that night he faced it "right on." He confessed. He repented, meaning he didn't want to go on living that way, and he was helped. Someone there in the church laid hands on him and prayed, and God delivered him, returning him to the way of joy and release.

When we face ourselves and bring our problem to God, we get release. But most of us have developed a habit pattern of getting *around* our guilt feelings. We pray or ask others to pray for us to relieve the symptoms, but nothing happens. Symptoms don't need to be relieved; sources need to be healed. And prayer is not to be used as an escape from the necessity for repentance from sin.

It is an interesting fact that the people who *don't* get healed at healing services are most often Christians. God is dealing with them, and they are trying to escape. God wants them to repent, and they want the symptoms to ease. No wonder Christians are confused, uneasy, and discontented. They've developed elaborate, impenetrable habit patterns of escape.

We're promised joy and peace in Jesus. If we don't have it we better take another look at the reason. The Apostle Paul says the kingdom of God is righteousness—then peace and joy (Rom. 14:17).

You can cheat on your income tax and carry resentment against your mother-in-law and still be a Christian. But you can't cheat on your taxes, resent your mother-in-law, and still have peace and happiness in your heart.

Once I was praying and telling God how much I loved Him and wanted to serve Him. I had just been discharged from the Navy and had been a Christian only a short time. The thought in my mind was unmistakably the voice of God: "Fine, son. Do you remember all that medicine you have stolen from the Navy?"

I had a regular little hospital at home, and I squirmed. "Yes, Lord."

"I want you to take it all back!"

"But God, if I take it back they'll send me to the penitentiary and I'll never get out."

"Pack it up and take it back!"

I packed two shopping bags full of medicine, medical instruments, bandages, and drugs and went to the Navy base. Walking up to the Officer of the Day, I said, "Sir, I have business with the Medical Officer."

The officer didn't even look in my shopping bags. He said, "Sign right here." I got through the gates and sank down on the curb, my stomach in a flutter.

"Thank you, Lord," I said, "for getting me through that gate."

I walked down the hall toward the Medical Officer's station, and a fellow called my name through an open door.

"Bob, where are you going?" I told him I had two shopping bags full of stolen articles and I was bringing them back.

"What's the matter with you!" he said amazed. "Everyone steals stuff like this from the Navy." I stayed and talked to him for two and a half hours about Jesus Christ and what He'd done in my life. Finally the fellow said, "I'm the civilian supply man. I'll put those things back on the shelves for you. You go home. Guys like you are dangerous to have around."

We put all the medicine back in proper order, and I walked out of that base floating on air. I thought if God can invade a Navy base like that, He can do anything. If I had refused to take the medicine back, I would have started a dangerous pattern of escape that would have led to negative spiritual symptoms and uselessness in God's kingdom.

Ask God to help you face yourself, to uncover your habit patterns and reveal your escape mechanisms and idiosyncrasies. We all have them. You will find God intruding into your daily life in a way that will keep you constantly on your toes.

One day I parked my car illegally, thinking I could get away with it. When I came back after a few minutes, there was a ticket. I said, "Lord, why didn't You protect me? I'm a minister and I work for You, Lord."

"Does that give you a license to break the law?" the Lord asked.

The next day, while I was driving home, the traffic light turned yellow. I sped up and flashed under it. Then I looked in the mirror. You guessed it. A patrol car was right behind me—his light blinking.

"God, what's the matter with You?" I murmured as I pulled to the curb. "I don't have the money to pay fines. I'm Your servant and would much rather give the money to missions than to the courts."

"Who do you think brought that patrol car?" the Lord responded. "Don't you understand what I'm trying to teach you?"

"Yes, Lord, I understand. Thank You for the ticket."

God won't permit escape mechanisms anymore. He wants to bring us to full release.

There are Christians who have escaped all their lives. They have never faced themselves, their marriage, or the Word of God. When the symptoms begin to pressure you in any area of your life, praise the Lord. God is presenting you an opportunity to face yourself. For unless you are willing to be honest with yourself, and with God, you cannot move on in God's plan for your life.

6

CONDITIONAL GUIDANCE

There is a fundamental difference between unconditional guidance and conditional guidance. The first is present in the lives of all believers. God acts in sovereignty regardless of *our* present attitude. A prime example is found in Isaiah 45. God says to Cyrus: "I will go before thee, and make the crooked places straight: I will break in pieces the gates of brass, and cut in sunder the bars of iron . . . For Jacob my servant's sake, and Israel mine elect, I have even called thee by thy name: I have surnamed thee, though *thou hast not known me*. I am the Lord, and there is none else, there is no God beside me: I girded thee though *thou hast not known me*" (Isa. 45:2,4–5).

Cyrus was king of Persia. In the Book of Ezra we read that in the first year of his reign God stirred up Cyrus's spirit so that he made a proclamation throughout all his reign saying that the Lord God of heaven had given him all the nations of the earth and charged him to build Him a house at Jerusalem. Cyrus then allowed all who were called "God's people" to go back to Jerusalem to rebuild the Temple. He told others to help with gifts of silver, gold, and freewill offerings for the house of God.

God was with Cyrus. He called him His shepherd who would perform all His pleasure. This was even before Cyrus knew God. Yet God's sovereign hand had begun to arrange the circumstances and lay all the nations under Cyrus's feet. Why did God do all this? Isa. 45:4 says it was, "For Jacob my servant's sake, and Israel mine elect." And Ezra adds additional perspective saying, "that the word of the Lord by the mouth of Jeremiah might be fulfilled" (Ezra 1:1).

God was using Cyrus to bring about the promise He had given His elect, Israel, through Jeremiah. Israel had been a rebellious, disobedient people, resisting God's guidance, seeking after other gods. As a result they were carried away captive to Babylon by Nebuchadnezzar. But through Jeremiah, God had spoken and said that after seventy years He would turn again their captivity, bring them back to Jerusalem, and rebuild the Temple. Had the Israelites obeyed God in the first place and turned from their wicked and rebellious ways when they were first warned through the words of the prophet, they would have escaped captivity. God was acting out His sovereign plan for the Israelites regardless of their attitude. This is *unconditional guidance.*

God's unconditional guidance is in operation in our lives because God honors His Word and because we are His people. It's not that we deserve it, but because Christ redeemed us on the Cross at Calvary.

It is significant that God had to use Cyrus, a foreign king, to guide His people back to Jerusalem. The Israelites, God's own people, didn't know the joy of walking in fellowship with God. They weren't listening to the Word of God, but Cyrus was.

How often do we find ourselves in the place where God wants us after having stumbled through a series of circumstances, grumbling all the way, completely oblivious of

God's hand? If we had listened to God in the first place, we would have gone joyfully, avoiding detours and painful delays.

Apart from God's unconditional guidance, there is also guidance that comes only when we comply with certain conditions. This is *conditional guidance* and is described in Isa. 58:10–11: "And if thou draw out thy soul to the hungry, and satisfy the afflicted soul; then shall thy light rise in obscurity, and thy darkness be as the noon day; And the Lord shall *guide thee continually,* and satisfy thy soul in drought, and make fat thy bones: and thou shalt be like a watered garden, and like a spring of water, whose waters fail not."

What would keep God from making good His promise of guiding us continually? If we don't draw out our soul to the hungry and don't satisfy the afflicted soul. God says there are certain conditions man must meet before he can receive specific guidance.

Selfishness is a hindrance to divine guidance. Selfishness produces a hardness in us of which He is constantly warning us. For example: the Holy Spirit urges us to give ten dollars to our unemployed friend.

"Not me, Lord. The kids need new shoes, and maybe I'll be laid off next." The point isn't the ten dollars. God could provide our friend with ten dollars from some other source. But a dangerous hardness develops in our spirit when we resist the leading of God. Therefore compassion becomes a requisite in our lives.

Stubbornness is another hindrance to guidance.

Psalm 32:8–9 reads: "I will instruct thee and teach thee in the way which thou shalt go: I will guide thee with mine eyes. Be ye not as the horse or the mule, which have no understanding: whose mouth must be held in with bit and bridle, lest they come near unto thee." There are many Christians who *know* what God wants of them but they refuse to obey. *A willingness to obey* is a primary condition for guidance. John 7:17 says: "If any man *will* do his will, he shall know of the doctrine, whether it be of God, or whether I speak of myself." Jesus reassures us that if we are willing to do God's will we'll not be led astray. I've heard people use the excuse, "I don't know if it is God's will or not." If you really are willing to do God's will, you'll know. Chances are there's a stubborn streak hidden somewhere, and the stubbornness is preventing you from doing what you ought to do. Stubbornness can prevent you from even seeking the will of God. Are you a "rugged individualist"? Stubborn individualists say, "I like my plans the way they are; I don't want God to interfere." There is a place for individuality, but in our relationship to God we must be yielded.

Disobedience also hinders guidance, that is, knowing unmistakably what God wants you to do, but refusing to do it. This is dangerous business, and the Bible is full of examples of what happened to men and women who deliberately hardened their hearts and set themselves to go against God's orders. The list is long and includes both the "enemies" of God as well as God's own people. You could begin with the first family on earth and see that original sin came into the world through a deliberate act of disobedience. Moses disobeyed when he smote the rock for water in the Desert of Zin. The Israelites disobeyed the command to go in and possess the land. Samson disobeyed and lost not only his strength, but his life. Saul disobeyed by consulting a witch, and the anointing of God was replaced with a curse. David deliberately committed adultery and murder and lost the joy of his salvation as well as the presence of the Holy Spirit. The list goes on and on, and the result of deliberate disobedience is always the same—the loss of God's conditional

guidance plus other penalties that suit the case. When God
says "Don't," we'd better not. When He says "Do," we'd
better. We have no one to blame but ourselves.

Insincerity stands between us and God's guidance.

There are people who pray loudly, "Oh God, I want to do
Your will. Just tell me Lord, and I'll do it." But in their
hearts they've got their course set and have no intention of
listening to God's advice.

The 42nd chapter of Jeremiah records the incident of the
remnant of Judah coming to Jeremiah and begging him to
seek the Lord for guidance. "Whatever God tells us to do,
we'll do," they said. Ten days later the word of God came to
Jeremiah, and he prophesied saying, "Don't go down to
Egypt. Stay here and God will prosper you. Go there and
you'll die by the sword and by famine and pestilence."

Did the leaders of Judah praise the Lord for His guidance? No. They turned against Jeremiah and said, "You're a
liar. That isn't what God says. We'll go to Egypt regardless!" They never intended to change their mind. They'd decided to go to Egypt and sent Jeremiah to seek God's Word
because they wanted His approval to do what they had already determined.

How many times have we done just that! We've decided
what we want to do, and we want to bolster our decision by
getting the approval of other Christians or the pastor. We
search the Bible for verses for support. We pray, "Oh, Lord,
show us the way," and seek the wise counsel of others. Then
if we run up against disapproval we say, "They just aren't
spiritual enough to understand God's will in this." We take
only the opinion and advice that agrees with our pre-set decision. That's insincerity. We didn't mean it when we asked
our Christian friends. We didn't mean it when we prayed.
Our insincerity and deceitfulness stand like a wall between
us and the guidance coming from God.

Impatience is another stumbling block.

Habakkuk 2:3 deals with this: "For the vision is yet for an appointed time, but at the end it shall speak, and not lie: though it tarry, wait for it; because it will surely come, it will not tarry."

A classic example of impatience interfering with God's guidance is found in I Sam. 13. Saul had been told to wait seven days before going into battle. At the end of this time Samuel was to appear and offer up a sacrifice to God. Seven days passed and Samuel didn't show up. Saul was impatient. He saw the enemy all around. His own troops were getting worried, and he decided to take matters into his own hands and go ahead with the sacrifice. No sooner had he done it, than Samuel came on the scene.

"Thou hast done foolishly," Samuel said to Saul. "Because of your impatience and foolishness God is going to take away your kingdom and give it to a man after God's own heart." Saul lost a kingdom because he didn't wait as he had been instructed.

Again and again in the Bible we are told that waiting on God is a necessity, a virtue, a source of strength. Yet impatience is probably the failure which occurs most often. We pray about a new job, the salvation of someone we love, the solution to a problem, and God gives us a wonderful assurance and peace. We know our prayers are being answered. We've got perfect peace—for an hour—but then we start nagging: "Lord, You promised. Why aren't You doing it, Lord?"

We busy ourselves arranging circumstances and manipulating people: "Lord, we've prayed for revival for a month. If You don't do something about it, we'll just go ahead and have a revival in our church anyway." We drum up a big campaign, hire an evangelist, and buy expensive advertising in the newspaper. When no one gets revived, and no one meets the Lord, we cry and moan: "Oh Lord, the hard hearts in the city just won't listen!"

God operates on split-second timing and He's never late. When the conditions are right and God's appointed time is here, God moves. By running ahead of Him we can seriously harm others and ourselves.

Once I prayed for a different car. I needed a more dependable one and God knew it. Day after day went by and I got impatient. Finally I decided I had waited long enough and marched into a used-car agency downtown:

"I'd like to look at a car," I said.

"Why certainly," the salesman said with a grin. "We'll fix you right up!"

He sure did. I had no peace when I looked at that car, but by then I was impatient, stubborn, *and* hard of hearing.

"I'll take it," I said and drove out. The car gave me nothing but trouble, and I was still making payments long after the car was hauled to the junkyard.

Perhaps the most dangerous hindrance to guidance is *self-sufficiency*.

By nature we say, "Show me and I'll believe."

God says, "Believe—and you'll see!"

Prov. 3:5–7 gives us this piece of advice: "Trust in the Lord with all thine heart; and lean not unto thine own understanding. In all thy ways acknowledge him, and he shall direct thy paths. Be not wise in thine own eyes: fear the Lord and depart from evil."

One of God's greatest enemies in His servants is self-sufficiency. Much of God's dealing with us is to destroy this. It manifests itself in this way: "You teach me, Lord, and I'll take it from there."

The life of dependence is humbling, and God keeps us in

a slight state of crisis at all times. An associate of mine who knows the life of dependency upon God recently needed $1,200. After much prayer and discipline in dependence, the money was remarkably supplied. He gave a heavy sigh of relief to which God responded, "Is this a sigh of relief because the money has been supplied—or because you no longer have to trust Me?" It was a rebuke well needed.

Pride is a real but subtle hindrance to guidance.

For years God dealt with me about becoming a Christian behind the steering wheel. I had always considered myself an expert driver and felt I didn't need any guidance from God on that score. Then one day I read a report by a trooper in the Canadian Royal Mounted Police that said most accidents were caused not by faulty brakes, speed, or even alcohol, but because most drivers subtly felt they were much better drivers than they were in reality. The trooper was saying that false pride led drivers to take chances and do unwise and unsafe things because of their blinding conceit which led them to say, "When I'm at the wheel everything is okay." Little by little God reduced my self-sufficiency and taught me to trust Him and His evaluation of every road situation.

Many people who have graduate degrees in psychology or engineering or medicine trust God in the "religious" areas of their life, that is, in going to church on Sunday, making moral decisions about lying or cheating, or even tithing their money. But when it comes to their own specialty—psychology, engineering, medicine—pride causes them to reject God's guidance.

God does not want us to be robots. He expects us to use our thinking processes. He longs for us to mature to the place that we can use our sanctified intellect and understanding to make the right decisions in following God's guidance. However, God knows infinitely more than we do about *any* given subject in which we may consider ourselves experts. His desire for us is that we acknowledge Him as sovereign God and recognize our own need for Him.

Ordinarily we think that the more we learn of God's ways the more we will be able to move with self-assurance and certainty. But actually the more we understand, the more dependent upon God we become.

Jeremiah cried out to God: "Oh Lord, I know that the way of man is not in himself: it is not in man that walketh to direct his steps" (Jer. 10:23). Jeremiah had come to recognize his own need, and this is a primary condition for direct guidance.

Pride is not willing to be taught. Only the meek can learn. Psalm 25:9 says: "The meek will he guide in judgment: and the meek will he teach his way."

When we depend solely on God in all areas of our life, He can meet our needs and guide us in all things. Only then can we surrender our wills completely to the will of God and say with David, "I delight to do thy will, my God: yea, thy law is within my heart" (Psa. 40:8).

The secret of the Christian life, says Paul, is that Christ lives within us. When Christ rules in our lives we should be able to say with him: "My meat is to do the will of him that sent me, and to finish his work" (John 4:34).

The characteristic of a *surrendered will* is a determination to set aside its own will for that of God. Jesus prayed in Gethsemane, "Father, if thou be willing, remove this cup from me: nevertheless not my will, but thine be done."

A completely yielded will opens the door for direct divine guidance in our lives.

CHAPTER

7

THREE HARBOR LIGHTS

A certain harbor in Italy can be reached only by sailing up a narrow channel between dangerous rocks and shoals. Over the years, many ships have been wrecked here, and navigation is extremely hazardous.

To guide the ships safely into port, three lights have been mounted on three huge poles in the harbor. When the three lights or poles are perfectly lined up and seen as one, the ship can safely proceed up the narrow channel. If the pilot sees two lights or three separately, he knows that he's off course and in danger!

For our safety in navigating our ships of life, God has provided three beacons to guide us. The same rules of navigation apply to us as to the harbor pilot. The three lights must be perfectly lined up as one before it is safe for us to proceed up the channel. The three harbor lights of guidance are:

1. The Word of God (objective standard)
2. The Holy Spirit (subjective witness)
3. Circumstances (divine providence)

Together they assure us that the directions we've received are from God and will lead us safely along the way that is His perfect will for us.

The written Word of God is the supreme criterion in guidance. In his second epistle, Peter refers to his experience on the Mount of Transfiguration with Jesus, James, and John. Here they saw Moses and Elijah and heard the voice of God from heaven say, "This is my beloved Son, in whom I am well pleased" (II Pet. 1:17).

Can you imagine what it would have been like to have been with Jesus on that mountaintop? Can you imagine what it would have been like to have seen Jesus transfigured before your eyes and to have heard the audible voice of God with your own ears? And yet Peter says, "We have also a *more sure word* of prophecy; whereunto ye do well that ye take heed, as unto a light that shineth in a dark place, until the day dawn, and the day star arise in your hearts: Knowing this first, that no prophecy of the scripture is of any private interpretation" (II Pet. 1:19–20). Peter had heard the audible voice of God from heaven, yet he says that the written Word is *more sure*.

The Bible is the Word of God. Jesus Himself said: "For verily I say unto you, Till heaven and earth pass, one jot or one tittle shall in no wise pass from the law, till all be fulfilled" (Matt. 5:18). He later said: "Heaven and earth shall pass away: but my words shall not pass away" (Luke 21:33).

The amazing thing about the Word of God is that it never goes out of style. Over the last decades we've seen the remarkable changes in concepts of science as research has uncovered evidence supporting the views of the Bible. Interesting, isn't it, that as man's empirical knowledge of his nature and environment increases, the gap of conflict between God's revelation in the Bible and man's knowledge narrows rather than widens. The concept that says, "We no longer accept or need a particular part of the Bible," simply cannot stand the close scrutiny of modern science.

The Bible is a *living* Word; the mere reading of it can quicken hearts, change lives, and heal broken bodies or spirits. Jesus, who is God's Word become flesh, uses the expression, "I am the vine, ye are the branches." I would like to use the same illustration about the written Word of God, the Bible. The first three chapters of Genesis make up the root of the vine. To cut off the root would mean the rest of the vine would wither and die. The whole Bible stands or falls on the story of the beginning. The same is true with the story of the beginning of the life of Jesus. To say it doesn't matter whether Jesus was born of a virgin or not is like cutting the taproot of the vine but still expecting a harvest of grapes in the fall. The Bible is an organic whole.

The Book of Corinthians was written in A.D. 56. That's over 1,900 years ago. What if you wanted to study electronics, automobile mechanics, medicine, or aerodynamics? Would you pick up a book written in A.D. 56? Of course not! You probably wouldn't even take seriously a textbook written fifty years ago. But the problems of the Corinthians are still applicable to us and our society, and so are the solutions. Thus the Word of God stands as a valid criterion for everything we do today. It does indeed speak to the whole of life.

Can God speak to us today? Of course He can. But how can we know it is God and not Satan or our own superheated imagination? By measuring God's spoken Word by His written Word.

Jesus spoke directly to his disciples, yet they always seemed to misunderstand Him. He became a little exasperated with them a few times because He had to tell them things over and over again and they still didn't understand what He meant. Once, when in a boat, He told the disciples, "Beware of the leaven of the Pharisees."

The disciples talked among themselves and decided that Jesus was disturbed because they had forgotten to bring bread. Jesus knew what they were thinking and said that wasn't what He meant at all; after all, didn't they remember how He had fed the five thousand with just a couple of loaves? At last the disciples understood what he meant: leaven was the dangerous doctrine of the Pharisees and Sadducees (Matt. 16:5–12).

Another time Jesus stood in front of the Temple and said, "If you destroy this temple, in three days I will raise it up." Again they misinterpreted completely what He said.

Several years ago I was riding in a car with a friend when the glory of God seemed to fill the entire car. We had been praying, praising, and worshiping as we drove along, and the Spirit of God was so real and overwhelming that we pulled over to the side and stopped. The atmosphere was supercharged with the wonderful presence of the Holy Spirit and the voice of the Lord was distinct in my mind: "I want you to go to Peru!"

It was a dramatic and direct call. *God wants me to go to Peru immediately*, I thought. My wife and I sold all our belongings, believing that God was going to miraculously supply the needed $5,000 so we could fly off to Peru and minister to the Indians. We waited week after week, but still no provisions arrived. It was seven years before the Lord brought me to Peru, and even then not as I had expected, but as an invited teacher for a ministers' training course.

God's revelation was only partial, but I was in such a hurry I acted as if it was complete. When I finally arrived in Peru and stood on a platform among the towering mountains of the Andes, I heard the voice of the Lord distinctly again: "Now you are seeing the fulfillment of My Words to you."

Standing there, I wept openly: "God, how I misinterpreted what you said to me!" God had given me the inner witness of the Holy Spirit, but I lacked the third witness, the open door of circumstances, and had almost wreaked havoc in my ministry by trying to run ahead of Him.

A Christian building contractor was talking on the telephone with another Christian friend. Suddenly the friend said, "It is the Lord's desire to bless you!" The contractor thought, *God intends to give me more money and prosper my business!* Thinking this was what "bless you" meant, he began to expand his construction business on every hand. He overextended himself financially and the bottom fell out. He was broke! He couldn't understand what had happened. Hadn't the Lord promised to bless him?

He concluded that he had no choice but to declare bankruptcy. The Lord's voice came through loud and clear, however: "Oh, no you're not. Stay with it. You aren't skipping out on a single debt. We'll pay them back together."

One by one, miraculously, God paid the bills. It took several years, but slowly the business gained until he was completely out of debt. Later he told me, "I am so thankful for what God has taught me over the last few years. He has truly blessed me."

Was it necessary for him to go through near bankruptcy to learn? Yes, but only because my friend didn't know how to measure what he had heard with the other two criteria of God's written Word and circumstances.

Most of us completely misunderstand what God says in the first place. We immediately jump to the wrong conclusion instead of waiting for the other two harbor lights to line up as witnesses to give solid guidance and direction.

Many problems in Christianity come because we read into God's Word something that isn't there. We get carried away by our own imaginations. Equally confusing, however, is the removal of portions of God's Word because it conflicts with our church tradition or dispensational teaching.

The three harbor lights are there because the passage is dangerous, with rocks and shoals on both sides. There are three sources of guidance: God, Satan, and our own super-heated spirit or imagination. We get all worked up, we hear and see things, and in this state we misinterpret and get ourselves into great difficulty.

Someone says, "I've had a vision; I've seen an angel!" This is quite possible, but could it be false? Are we supposed to follow every vision and listen to every angel?

In I Cor. 14:37 Paul says, "If any man think himself to be a prophet, or spiritual, let him acknowledge that the things that I write unto you are the commandments of the Lord." The Holy Spirit himself yields to and bows to the written Word. He never acts outside of or in contradiction to the Word of God. This is His own criterion so that we can recognize what is of God and what is not. He, the Holy Spirit, is the one who *inspired* the Word of God in the first place.

I have met people in Christian circles who have had weird visions and messages. If I try to speak to them about it, they bristle and back up like porcupines.

"Are you challenging what God said to me?"

"Yes; what about *this* verse?"

"I can't help what that verse says, I only *know* what God said to me!"

God never speaks in contradiction to His own written Word. He will never lead you beyond the revelation He has already given in Jesus Christ. Don't ever move because of one initial leading. If it is God speaking to you, the other two lights will line up in perfect agreement—and God never expects you to move without waiting for that assurance. There is a law in the scriptures saying that a thing is established by two or three witnesses. If a man was caught in adultery and there were two or three witnesses, he was stoned without discussion. In guidance we need the three witnesses to be sure: the Word, the inner witness of the Holy Spirit, and outward circumstances. Either of the three taken alone can be deceptive. Wait for all three to line up. The Word of God never lies, but a verse lifted out of context can lead us astray.

There are three forms of effortless guidance which, although not to be discounted as possible legitimate forms, are the kind that will turn us into spiritual pigmies. Their quick and easy approach leads us into the dangerous habit of bypassing the serious effort we need to put forth to find genuine guidance. I refer to them as *finger pointing, button pushing*, and *promise card dealers*.

Let me hasten to add that I know these three forms of guidance have worked under certain circumstances and in certain occasions, but I say unequivocally that a continued dependence upon them will result in deception.

Let us look at *finger pointing*. A young couple who felt called to the mission field and didn't know where to go, opened their Bible at random, pointed at a verse and read, "The isles of the sea wait for thee."

They said, "That means the Lord wants us to go to one of the Pacific islands."

Six months later they were back. The wife spent some time in a mental institution and they were both broken in faith and spirit.

An equal danger lies in *button pushing*. I worked with a doctor in Toronto who had a patient who believed she had cancer—even though she didn't. The doctor, however, treated her and counseled her.

After she left I said, "You're deceiving her."

"No, she's a button pusher," he said. "That means if I don't treat her for what she thinks she has she'll keep ringing doctors' doorbells until she hears what she wants to hear. Thus I give her harmless treatments through deception while someone else would have taken advantage of her."

Sincere but careless Christians often feel guidance can be obtained by asking (button-pushing) a variety of spiritual leaders, pastors, and visiting evangelists. Often, they keep asking until someone tells them what they want to hear.

The same danger lies in using a *promise box* for guidance. A box of scriptures is a good thing to have on the breakfast table and makes for uplifting and pleasant devotion. But used in guidance it has dangerous potential. God's promises are all real, but picked out of context from a promise box they *can* be misleading.

Maybe one day you're crying out to God because you have many needs: the rent is due and the grocery bill unpaid. You reach into the box for a promise. There it is, thank God: "But my God shall supply all your need according to his riches in glory by Christ Jesus." Hallelujah, you have nothing to worry about! Just wait, and the Lord will do it.

But wait a minute! In what context did Paul assure the Philippians of God's willingness to supply all their needs? Paul had just received their liberal gifts and tithes. The Philippians had done what was required of them; they had met God's condition. Have you? Perhaps the guidance you needed that morning was from Prov. 3:9–10: "Honor the Lord with thy substance, and with the firstfruits of all thine increase: So shall thy barns be filled with plenty, and thy presses shall burst out with new wine."

Some people read the most amazing things into the Word

of God. I remember hearing about a boy who wanted to marry a girl named Grace. He prayed God would show him if she was the right one. He opened his Bible to Phil. 1:2 and read, "Grace be unto you, and peace, from God our Father, and from the Lord Jesus Christ." What a flimsy foundation for guidance to enter into the implications of lifelong marriage.

Past experience had taught me not to rush ahead of God and buy a new car out of season, but there came a time when I was in real need of means of transportation. I prayed, "Lord only when it's Your perfect timing do I want a car. Even then You'll have to find it for me and make all the circumstances fall into place."

That morning I read in my Bible, "Delight thyself also in the Lord, and he shall give thee the desires of thine heart" (Psa. 37:4). Now the Lord knew that one of the desires of my heart was for a new car, so I said, "Praise You Lord; I'll just delight myself in You and not worry about the rest."

Later, that same day, I was driving down the road and spotted a neat little car sitting in the lot next to a service station. I felt a tugging in my spirit.

"That's the one!"

I stopped and asked the man to let me look at the car. A quiet sense of peace in my spirit told me the car was for me.

"All right, Lord," I said, a little excited. "I see two signs: Your word this morning and now Your Holy Spirit telling me to buy this car, but I'm going to wait until the circumstances line up. You'll have to sell my old car before I can buy this one."

By now I was getting a little more excited. I had watched two lights line up and I was waiting for the third. I went home, called a man on the phone, and he bought my old car for cash. Praise the Lord! That was the third light.

I purchased the car, and by the time I'd put 50,000 miles on it, it still had cost me only forty dollars in repairs, quite unlike the one I bought outside of God's will, which cost me a fortune in repair bills.

When the three harbor lights of guidance line up, God is making His will evident. We can always rely on this. God's guidance is not a shadowy, haphazard thing. It is certain— and can become working knowledge in our lives.

8

ABIDING IN THE WORD!

From where do you expect your guidance to come?

In the days of Moses, God led his children through the desert by some pretty spectacular means. There was the pillar of smoke by day, fire by night, and the voice of God thundered to Moses on the mountain. Perhaps, we think, if we get to be spiritual enough, that will happen to us as well?

No, I think that highly unlikely. Let me nail something down very firmly. It is my personal conviction that some seventy percent of our guidance comes through the written Word of God, approximately another twenty percent comes by the Holy Spirit speaking, and the last ten percent may come through dreams, visions, prophecy, or other direct signs. It is when we make the *exception* to be the *norm* that difficulties arise.

Jesus was quite specific in his instructions to those who believe on Him: "If you abide in My Word—hold fast to My teachings and live in accordance with them—you are truly My disciples" (John 8:31 *Amplified Bible*).

No team of scientists in their right minds would attempt to construct a rocket and send it to the moon without thoroughly acquainting themselves with all the available data on rocket building and space travel. No team of doctors would undertake open-heart surgery without being thoroughly acquainted with every available knowledge and skill in that area.

The Word of God in the Bible is just as essential for our survival as Christians looking for God's direct guidance in our lives. Studying the Bible is a lifetime project. In fact, the more mature we become as Christians the more we need to study it. Yet there are some Christians who either feel they've "arrived" or admit they are too busy doing "God's Work" and say they don't need to read it. We *must* read it and know it, for in the Bible is the key to our knowledge of the character and nature of God as well as the key to understanding our own character and nature. It is the first of the three harbor lights of God's guidance.

How does the Word of God guide?

"Every Scripture is God-breathed—given by His inspiration—and profitable for instruction, for reproof and conviction of sin, for correction of error and discipline in obedience, and for training in righteousness [that is, in holy living, in conformity to God's will in thought, purpose and action], So that the man of God may be complete and proficient, well-fitted and thoroughly equipped for every good work" (II Tim. 3:16–17 *Amplified Bible*).

There may be areas in our lives where we are uncertain; we don't know what to do or what God wants of us. However, if we knew His written Word, if we allowed His Word to become part of our flesh, deeply rooted in our being, we would *know* what to do in many areas where we now vacillate back and forth.

There is an interesting comment on this in Prov. 11:3: "The integrity of the upright shall guide them; but the perverseness of transgressors shall destroy them." Webster defines "integrity" as a "state or quality of being complete, undivided or unbroken, entirety. An unimpaired state; soundness, purity. Moral soundness; honesty; uprightness."

It is interesting that integrity is a state of being *complete* just as we read in II Timothy. If we allow the scriptures to instruct us, convict us of sin, correct us, discipline us, and train us in righteousness, we may become *complete. Integrity* is impossible to achieve, however, without knowing and obeying the principles of the Word of God.

The Word of God guides in that it *reproves* from wrongdoing. It tells us how to dress, where to go, and where not to go. I don't have to stand outside a theatre showing a pornographic film and ask, "Lord, should I go in or shouldn't I?" It is perfectly clear in the Word of God that I should not.

I want to sound a word of warning here. The person who prays for guidance when he *already knows* the answer, opens himself for deception! Suppose I find a wallet in an empty church pew. Inside I find $750. Should I pray, "Jesus, is it Your will that I keep this money—or should I return it?" The very fact that I even ask such a question indicates I desire to be deceived. It follows that I may hear a voice that urges me to keep it.

I know a young couple who got in trouble this way. They were very much in love. Both were Christians, filled with the Spirit, and they wanted to serve God together. They were going to be married but hadn't set the date yet. Tragically, however, one day they were alone in her apartment and were overcome by their passion for each other. They got to their knees in the bedroom and prayed, "Lord, if it is Your will that we make love now before we're married, keep anybody from knocking on our door this afternoon. If it is against Your will that we do this, Lord, please send somebody to knock on the door right now, and we'll take that as a sign." Nobody came to the door, and the young couple went ahead with their lovemaking. Later they experienced much depression and confusion and just couldn't understand why. After all, hadn't they asked God to stop them if He wanted to? It was God's fault, not theirs.

When you pray for something God has already forbidden in His Word, you're likely to get your guidance from the wrong source.

I know married people who've been led into adultery the same way. There are Spirit-baptized Christians who feel God led them into an adulterous relationship. They were so blinded by their love and hunger for companionship, they claimed they had asked God's guidance every step of the way. Somewhere along that way they must have listened to another voice. God's Word is very plain, and He doesn't change His basic principles. Adultery is sin, and God would never, never lead you to sin.

I know a young lady who prayed for the Lord to show her whom she was to marry. One day in church she looked up at her pastor who was preaching and heard a little voice saying, "He's the one!" She responded with gratitude. She accepted that guidance and began her program of accomplishment. Had she known and obeyed the Word of God she would have rejected that little voice, because the pastor was already married. Yet for several years that young lady considered herself "spiritually engaged" and suffered increasing agonies over her "love." She finally came to a Christian counselor for help, but even then refused to acknowledge that her first "revelation" could be false. She was convinced that the love she felt for her married pastor was given to her by God, even though it was ripping her apart emotionally. Had she known that the wisdom that comes from above is first pure, peaceable, and gentle (James 3:17), she could have evaluated her guidance accordingly.

When we pray for guidance over things like that—"Lord are you sure that man is your choice for me?" "Should I keep that wallet, Lord?"—we open ourselves to deception. To pray over such things or even to weigh them in your mind invites trouble.

When false guidance like that comes, we have the Word of God to correct us. Prayer or rationalization is unnecessary because we *know* from the Word of God that we are not supposed to covet our friend's husband or steal our neighbor's wallet. Praying for guidance when we already know the answer is like a burglar who prays, "Lord, if You want me to pull that holdup in the bank, keep the police away. If You don't want me to steal, let a police car come by right now."

In the Book of Numbers there is a fascinating story about a prophet who prayed for guidance when he knew already what God wanted him to do. The Moabites and Midianites asked Balaam, the prophet, to curse the Israelites. When Balaam sought God's will, he was told not to curse the Israelites. A second time the Moabites and Midianites came to Balaam. This time they offered him many riches if he would curse the Israelites. Thinking about all that money (and how it could be used for the kingdom's work), Balaam asked God for advice again. This time God said, "Go with them, but speak only as I give you words."

Delighted over his guidance, Balaam went. However, God sent an angel to stand in his way with a drawn sword. Balaam was riding on an ass, and even though the angel was invisible to Balaam, the ass could see him standing before him in the road. When the ass refused to go on, Balaam became very angry. He hit the ass, and this is when the ass opened its mouth and God spoke through the animal.

Balaam's end was a sad one. He became a false prophet

who led many astray and was finally slain by the Israelites.

Peter, Jude, and Revelation all warn against falling into his way, error, and doctrine. "The *integrity* of the upright shall guide them . . ." (Prov. 11:3).

The Bible is full of examples of this kind of guidance. In II Sam. 24 we find King David coming to Araunah asking to buy his threshing place. God had told him through the prophet Gad to *buy* the place and build an altar there. Araunah offered to *give* David the threshing-floor with oxen for burnt sacrifice and the threshing instruments for wood. But David had learned a lesson. Earlier in the chapter it's recorded how David had sinned, repented, and God had given him three choices of how his sin might be paid for: "Shall seven years of famine come unto thee in thy land? or wilt thou flee three months before thine enemies while they pursue thee? or that there be three days' pestilence in thy land?" David chose not to become the prey of his enemies, and so God sent pestilence on the land and seventy thousand men died.

By now David has seen his selfishness, that he had allowed the innocent to die for his own sins. He cried out to God: "Lo, I have sinned and I have done wickedly: but these sheep, what have they done? Let thine hand, I pray thee, be against me, and against my father's house."

No longer does David want others to pay for his sins or his sacrifices. Guided by his new sense of *integrity* he says to Araunah: "Nay, but I will surely buy it of thee at a price: Neither will I offer burnt offering unto the Lord my God of that which doth cost me nothing."

Integrity was also the guide for Abram who refused to take any spoils of war for himself. The story is found in Genesis 14. The kings of Sodom and Gomorrah had been taken captive by the enemy. Captured along with them was Lot and all his goods. When Abram heard that his nephew had been taken away captive, he armed his 318 servants and went after the enemy. He defeated them in battle and brought back all the goods and the people, including Lot.

The High Priest and king of Salem (later Jerusalem), Melchizedek, brought Abram bread and wine and blessed him, saying, "Blessed be Abram of the most high God, possessor of heaven and earth: And blessed be the most high God, which hath delivered thine enemies unto thy hand." Abram gave Melchizedek a tenth of everything he had brought back from the battle. The king of Sodom then asked Abram to release to him the persons he had rescued from the enemy kings. In return, he would let Abram keep all the goods for himself. But Abram refused, saying, "I have lift up mine hand unto the Lord, the most high God, the possessor of heaven and earth, That I will not take from a thread, even to a shoelatchet, and that I will not take any thing that is thine, lest thou shouldest say, I have made Abram rich."

The *integrity* of Abram caused him to recognize that God had won the battles against the enemy. Abram couldn't have done it on his own. Also, he saw that God alone is the source of his riches, not the king of Sodom. We all know the end of the story for Sodom. Because of the great wickedness of the people, God destroyed the city. Now if you or I had been in Abram's shoes, what would we have done? After all, didn't we risk our life and limb and all our trained servants to rescue the captives and the goods from the enemy? If that wicked king of Sodom wanted to give us some gold, silver, cattle, and goods as a token of his gratitude, what harm would there be in taking it? Abram was dwelling in the poor hill-country and the king of Sodom had plenty of fertile land in the valley. He could well afford to part with some of his goods.

The integrity of Abram was his guide. He took only what God gave him, lest a man should brag and say, "I made Abram rich." God had promised Abram riches, and Abram didn't want anyone to doubt the source. He wanted to be able to say with a clear conscience, "The Lord has blessed me and kept His promises unto me."

Boaz was another who was guided by *integrity* in a tricky situation. Remember how Ruth came to glean corn in his field. Ruth was a young widow and her widowed mother-in-law told her that Boaz was a near kinsman of Ruth's deceased husband. According to Jewish law and custom, it was the duty and legal right of a man to marry the widow of his deceased brother—making sure she would have a child to carry on the deceased brother's name. This duty extended to the next kinsman in line if the first one refused.

Boaz had seen Ruth in the field and was attracted to her. Thus, on her mother-in-law's advice she went to the threshing-floor where Boaz was sleeping. She lay down at his feet. Startled, Boaz awoke:

"Who's there?" he cried out.

Shyly, Ruth told him who she was and that she had come to him because he was a near kinsman.

Boaz knew that Ruth was a virtuous woman who had come to him in good faith. He was pleased, for he had already fallen in love with her the first time he saw her—which really complicated matters in his mind. But Boaz also knew that there was another man in the city who was an even closer kinsman to Ruth than himself. This man had the legal right ahead of Boaz to take Ruth as his wife.

It was a tight spot to be in. Ruth was there, waiting for him to take her as his wife. He had already fallen in love with her. No one would ever know the difference. Besides, she was a gentile and no Jew would want her—or so he hoped. Yet Boaz was guided by his *integrity*. He knew the law and told Ruth that first he must go to this other man and inform him of his rights. If he didn't want to exercise them, then Boaz could take Ruth for his wife.

Ruth lay at his feet till morning and slipped away before anyone could see that she had been there. Boaz went to see the other man, who turned down his rights to marry Ruth, leaving Boaz free to claim her as his own. They had a son named Obed who had a son named Jesse who was the father of David.

Integrity guided Joseph in Egypt when he was overseer in the house of the captain of the guard. Potiphar had trusted everything he owned into the hands of Joseph whom he had bought as a slave. But when Potiphar's wife came after Joseph and asked him to go to bed with her, he turned her down.

"Your husband has trusted everything he owns to me," he said. "How can I do this great wickedness and sin against God?"

Scorned, Potiphar's wife accused Joseph of raping her and he wound up in a prison dungeon. But that's where he met Pharaoh's chief butler who in turn told Pharaoh that Joseph could interpret dreams. When Joseph interpreted Pharaoh's dreams about the seven rich years and the seven lean years of famine to follow, Pharaoh made him ruler over all Egypt. Joseph could have worked ten lifetimes trying to climb the social ladder in Egypt and never gained what those few years in prison brought him. Such is the reward of integrity.

Personal integrity was the guide for these men of God in the Bible. And their integrity was based on a thorough knowledge of the Word of God and the character of God as it is revealed in His Word and His Law. Personal integrity based on an intimate knowledge of the Word of God is a basic avenue of guidance. All other guidance goes on from there, but without this foundation we can never fully enter into God's perfect will and plan for our individual lives.

9

THE HOLY SPIRIT SPEAKS

The second of the three harbor lights of guidance is the inner witness of the Holy Spirit. In the Book of Acts we find many examples of this. One example appears in Acts 8:29: "Then the Spirit said unto Philip, Go near and join thyself to this chariot."

My question is, How did the Holy Spirit speak to Philip? Was it an audible voice? Was it something within Philip's spirit? We aren't told how the Spirit spoke, yet Philip knew the words and obeyed.

Men whom I trust, scholarly, Bible-believing men, have heard God speak in an audible voice. Such was the experience of young Samuel with Eli in the Temple (I Sam. 3:10). Although I have never heard God speak in an audible voice, I have heard Him speak distinct words deep inside me. In Colombia, South America, I was lying upon my bed when the presence of the Lord came into the room and the Holy Spirit said very distinctly, "I want you to go back to school!"

It couldn't have been any clearer if my wife had spoken the words right next to me. It was spoken straight and strong and right into my spirit. It wasn't a demanding, urgent voice. If it had been, I would immediately have suspected the source to be someone or something other than the Lord. The vocal impression was warm, but firm. I knew it was the Lord.

In Chapter 1 we discussed James's characteristics of wisdom coming from God contrasted with the wisdom coming from below. The wisdom from above is always peaceable and pure. When God speaks, there is always a sense of peace deep within our spirit, even if we don't like what He's saying.

I didn't like it when I was told to go back to school. I had already graduated from one Bible college. I had a wife and children to support, and I argued with the Holy Spirit. Three days later, however, there were further instructions: "I want you to go to The Reformed Episcopal Seminary in Philadelphia, Pennsylvania."

It didn't seem logical for a Spirit-filled Bible teacher to go back to seminary, but the voice that spoke to my spirit was indeed the voice of God. He didn't speak to my mind, emotions, or will. Rather He spoke to my inner being—that *me* which is spirit alone. And so I said, "Lord, I'm willing. Now arrange the circumstances."

He did, and we went. Many times across the years we have seen the fruit of our obedience.

The Holy Spirit can and does speak sometimes in distinct, understandable words. On occasion this may be external and audible, but this is the exception. Most often it is internal, subjective, but perfectly clear and distinct. Receiving guidance depends greatly on our ability to recognize the voice of God when He speaks to us. It was important for Philip to recognize and obey when the Holy Spirit spoke to him. It is important that we do too.

Our textbook for this kind of direct guidance is the Book of Acts. Here we find countless examples of the Holy Spirit giving specific instructions to the disciples: "Go here—don't go there." Earlier Jesus himself had told the disciples where to go and what to do. Jesus told his disciples that He would soon go to the Father, but that they should not grieve: "I assure you that it is a good thing for you that I should go away. For if I did not go away, the divine helper would not come to you. But if I go, then I will send him to you. . . . he will guide you into everything that is true" (John 16:7,13 Phillips).

After Jesus' resurrection, He showed himself to the disciples, and before His ascension He emphasized that they were to stay in Jerusalem and wait for the fulfillment of the promise: "Before many days are passed you will be baptized with the Holy Spirit . . . you are to be given power when the Holy Spirit has come to you" (Acts 1:5,8 Phillips).

At Pentecost, tongues of fire descended from heaven and the assembled followers of Jesus Christ were baptized in the Holy Spirit, just as He had promised. This introduced the disciples into a brand-new realm of experiencing the presence and power of God. It also opened them to the influence of other spiritual powers, and in reading the Book of Acts we see how the disciples had to *learn the skill* of knowing the voice of God, often by trial and error.

In our lives the baptism in the Holy Spirit opens the door for us to receive God's power. It is our tool-kit, but we must learn to use it. This can be likened to learning to play the piano or the accordion or learning to use the typewriter. At first you hunt and peck, thinking you'll never learn. A sense of failure or inability nags until you pass a certain point at which time faith responds and you realize that you can— you will be able to learn.

On several occasions I have followed what I thought was the leading of the Holy Spirit only to find myself in a blind alley.

"Go down this street; there's a brick house on the right. Go there. The man needs Jesus." I drive down the street but there's no brick house! However, I'm learning! And at least I'm willing to be obedient and am encouraged by the fact that the disciples didn't *always* recognize the leading of God either.

Often we find that the Holy Spirit *restrains* us from a certain action. This wouldn't be necessary if we went in the right direction in the first place. The apostles, being human, had the same experiences. Paul and Silas were on their way through Phrygia and Galatia, "but the Holy Spirit prevented them from speaking God's message in Asia" (Act 16:6 Phillips).

It seems strange that the Holy Spirit would ever forbid anyone to preach the Good News anywhere. Shouldn't we preach the Word to everyone, everywhere?

No, there is a time to speak and a time to refrain from speaking. This is especially good advice for people who try to cram religion down everybody's throat.

"But I feel led to stand on the street corner and preach about Jesus Christ," one man told me. "I ask everybody who comes by if he knows Jesus as his Savior."

That's good IF the Holy Spirit commissioned you to do it. But if you're down there on the corner because you have a strong urge inside you, no peace, and you've got to do *something* to satisfy your restlessness, then it isn't the Holy Spirit's direction. It's simply your own undisciplined human spirit. Such "ministry" does incalculable harm to the spreading of the gospel. God knows the perfect timing. He knows when hearts and minds are tender and ready to receive His Word. When *He* sends you, people listen and a harvest is reaped.

A few years back there was a visitation of the Holy Spirit

in a Midwestern town. During a meeting the Holy Spirit fell on the congregation. The visitation spread through the city, and every day the minister of the church and the evangelist went to visit people in their homes or places of business. They drove down the street praying, praising the Lord, and waiting for the gentle tugging of the Holy Spirit who said: "Stop at *this* gas station, go in *here* for a cup of coffee, drive into *that* car lot, speak to *that* man . . ."

Every single person they spoke to either received Jesus Christ as his personal Savior or experienced the baptism in the Holy Spirit. Most of us, however, are so dense that God has to start leading us through *negative* or *restrictive* guidance.

"Don't speak the word in Asia!"

When Paul and Silas came to Mysia they tried to enter Bithynia, "but again the Holy Spirit wouldn't permit them." They still didn't know where God wanted them to go. They wanted to get at the teeming millions of Asia, but God said "no." He was leading them by restrictive guidance.

I once thought that Paul, Silas, and the other apostles wore halos over their heads. I thought they were able to discern instantly what God wanted them to do. I was glad when I discovered in practice this wasn't the case.

In Bible college I had a professor whom I respected greatly. Once in class he told us, "This morning I got up to pray and I fell asleep!"

Spontaneously I said out loud, "Glory!"

Everybody in the class turned to look at me. The professor grinned and said, "What's the matter, Mr. Mumford? Are you glad to find out that I'm human?"

Embarrassed, I confessed, "To tell you the truth, sir, I am. I sometimes fall asleep during my morning prayer time, but I didn't think anybody else did."

When I first started listening to the prompting of the voice within, I often went in the wrong direction, but I wasn't aware that anybody else did. I was relieved when I discovered that Paul and Silas and the other apostles had the same problem. So do our present-day spiritual "giants"!

Remember the occasion when the disciples crossed the Sea of Galilee and Jesus said, "Beware of the leaven of the Pharisees"?

Reasoning among themselves as to what He meant, one of the disciples said, "He must have forgotten the lunch." This, of course, had nothing to do with what Jesus was seeking to impart. Their inability to perceive is comforting to me in two ways. One, it shows that all good disciples are a little thick and, two, that the Master is always rich in patience as He teaches us His ways. In fact, it's because of our thickness that God is forced to use more dramatic forms of guidance (visions) to impress His will upon us.

What would have happened if Paul had persisted in going into Asia? Possibly, the whole course of history could have been changed by this one man's failure to follow his guidance. Paul wasn't able to discern *where* God wanted him to go, but he did know God wanted him to go somewhere. He probably reasoned: "There's a real need in Asia, I think I'll go there." How did the Holy Spirit restrain him? It may have been by an audible voice, but more likely it was by upsetting Paul's peace. He tried preaching in Asia, but suddenly the peace of God inside was upset, and he knew he was on the wrong track. This trial-and-error method continued until Paul finally was in position to hear the positive guidance of the Holy Spirit.

There are people who sit still waiting for God to speak. "God, if you want me to go to church this Sunday, speak to me." But God wants us on the move. It is very difficult to turn the steering wheel on a stopped car. Get it moving and you can turn the wheel easily. Likewise, you can turn the helm of a docked ship, but nothing happens. It's only when the ship is on the move that it responds to the helmsman's touch on the wheel.

If I can't seem to get any direct guidance from God about where I'm to go or what I'm to do next, I use my best judgment, my sanctified intellect, and get moving. I've already surrendered my will to God and asked Him to lead me or restrict me if I'm heading the wrong way. I keep my inward ear listening for the prompting of the Spirit, and as I go I let Him guide.

Several years ago we moved to a new city and started a search for a church in which to worship. The Lord had not given any direct guidance. We visited one church, but there was no peace. Then another, still no peace. Finally, a third: Glory! The peace of God began flowing like a river.

I could have given up after the first two tries and said, "Lord, I tried two churches and You didn't tell me anything so I'm just going to sit here and wait until You let me know where to go." It is not that there was anything wrong with the first two churches, but God had a specific plan and place for us, as He does for each one.

A young man who showed great promise in school graduated from Bible college with me. He was married, had three children, and was living in one of the small cottages provided for married students. A couple of months after graduation I went to see him.

"What are your plans?" I asked.

He said, "Well, I haven't had any leadings from the Lord, so I'm just going to stay right here until Jesus tells me what to do." And there he sat until the "unspiritual" faculty helped him move out to give room to another family just starting to school.

"What should he have done?" you ask. Even without *specific* leading he could have used his sanctified intellect and at least begun to *move*.

"I'll find a home for my family and start traveling as an evangelist . . ." If he received negative guidance from the Lord he could have changed directions. "I'll find employment and at least assume the responsibility of providing for my family." That's one thing he could be sure God wanted him to do. If you walk in the little light you have, God will always supply more light.

As long as you move with a sincere desire to do God's will, He will guide you into the right place. But if you sit still and try to sweat God out, you'll find that He will not yield. I've tried it!

God will not be manipulated, and it's useless to try to figure Him out. Guidance involves principles to be learned —not techniques to be mastered.

I once knew a fellow who wanted to learn all about healings. He studied every incident of healing in the New Testament. He thought that by figuring out the *technique* Jesus and the disciples used, he would tap the secret of their power. Much to his dismay he discovered there weren't two healings alike. The only common denominator was dependence upon the Father—which, incidentally, is the secret of the power of our Lord Jesus Christ.

Guidance is like that. Learning to discern the voice of God is a skill, and it can be learned, but there are no two circumstances alike.

When the Holy Spirit speaks He may speak in positive guidance, or He may use negative guidance. And negative guidance, which often manifests itself by the disruption of inner peace, may be a preventive guidance to keep us away from harm which we'll never know about (unless we fail to heed the guidance).

While I was Dean of a Bible college in New York, my wife and I started on a trip to Delaware to interview some prospective students. We hadn't planned the trip or prayed about it. The farther I drove down the freeway, the more upset I became deep inside.

"Lord, what's the matter?" I asked.

Inside I felt the response, "You'd better stop right now."

I said to my wife, "Honey, do you sense something wrong?"

She said, "I certainly do." I put on the brakes and pulled over to the side of the road.

"Let's just stop and see what happens," I said. As soon as we stopped the car, the unrest and heaviness lifted. I said, "Thank You, Jesus," and turned the car around.

When we started back in the other direction, the glory of the Lord filled that car, and we began to worship Him. What had we been heading for? God only knows. But whatever it was, God's negative guidance had disquieted my peace and warned me not to go farther. It is important that we learn to recognize the restraining hand of God.

Sometimes we wonder if the negative guidance could be Satan's method of keeping us from doing God's will. Remember, though, that Satan cannot imitate the peace of God. When that peace is disturbed, take care.

We may hear an inner voice saying, "You're not praying enough. You need to pray more." Surely, Satan wouldn't tell you to pray! Sure he would. There are two ways Satan can trap us: either by leading us into obvious worldly sin or by pushing us overboard on some spiritual tangent. Sometimes God wants us to act—not pray. Satan can quote scripture also, talking about spiritual things, impressing upon us great religious fervor.

I counseled with a lady who had come under counterfeit

spiritual pressure. Voices were telling her to fast and pray, deprive herself of sleep, wear long black dresses, never read the newspaper or listen to musical instruments. She was under great duress, and she was forced to take another look and see that even "spiritual" guidance can come from Satan.

One way we can tell the difference between the voice of God and a counterfeit is the sense of peace. The voice which speaks peace is of God; the voice which speaks urgency is either of Satan or comes from your own human nature. God leads, Satan pushes.

The demanding voice says, "Quit your job right now. Don't wait for tomorrow. You're disobedient if you don't!" If we follow such advice we're in trouble, because God seldom speaks like that except in emergencies.

The Greek word for god is *theos*. This is the same root that our word "enthusiasm" comes from. The ancient Greeks looked at someone who was *entheos* as someone who was possessed by a god and transported into ecstasy. We need to recognize the fine line between genuine spiritual enthusiasm (which like deep water in a river may run fast but without froth and foam) and a kind of demonizing that leads us to frantically play the role of a religious cheerleader without any inner peace. As far as I am concerned, enthusiasm in religious realms *can* be a symptom of spiritual disease. Such things as loyalty-days, campaigns, competitions, and even "revivals" can take the place of genuine biblical vision and spiritual motivation. Building programs and personalities are not an adequate substitute for the presence of God to keep God's people "enthusiastic" about "religious things." Mountain peaks of enthusiasm can be just as dangerous as deep valleys in our walk with God.

When we come to know the abiding peace of God deep

in our spirit we have reached a balance and a stability that cannot be upset by circumstances or urgent voices speaking to our mind or emotions. Nor can we be fooled by counterfeit guidance, because we've learned to recognize the voice of God. Receiving divine guidance involves learning certain principles.

There are multitudes of people who have come into a relationship with Jesus Christ and been baptized in the Holy Spirit, but they go through life without practicing and developing the skill of following God's daily leading. They are like one who receives as a gift, a beautiful concert piano, but is satisfied to play with only one finger.

The baptism in the Holy Spirit, potentially, brings with it the promise of divine guidance, but we must understand the need for practice and development in receiving it. The author of Hebrews writes: "At a time when you should be teaching others, you need teachers yourselves to repeat to you the ABC of God's revelation to men. You have become people who need a milk diet and cannot face solid food! For anyone who continues to live on milk is obviously immature —he simply has not grown up. 'Solid food' is only for the adult, that is, for the man *who has developed by experience* his power to discriminate between what is good and what is bad for him" (Heb. 5:14 Phillips).

The only way to develop the ability to discriminate between the voice of God and other voices is by *experience*, by use. There are many voices clamoring for our attention. More than ever before in history it is important that we learn to know the Voice of God.

10

THE PEACE OF GOD

We have mentioned the activity of the Holy Spirit as the subjective witness speaking to our spiritual man. This voice is the active function of the Holy Spirit. The second function, equally important, is the passive aspect of the ministry of the Holy Spirit known as the Peace of God.

Few words are as misunderstood and abused today as PEACE. We see it painted on signs and fences; riots and protest marches are carried on under its banner; bumper-stickers read PEACE NOW next to a symbol called the "peace sign." (That upside-down broken cross within a circle, incidentally, was designed in the first century and used during witches' masses to signify the power of Satan over the broken power of Jesus Christ).

The peace of God in guidance functions according to the principle outlined in Col. 3:15: "Let the peace (soul harmony which comes) from the Christ rule (act as umpire continually) in your hearts—deciding and settling with finality all questions that arise in your minds—[in that peaceful state] to which [as members of Christ's] one body you were also called [to live]" (*Amplified Bible*).

This means that the peace of God is to act as umpire, witness within us for or against an intended course of action. This is an important aspect of any subjective guidance.

How does the peace of God do this? It occurs when we have conscious rest or assurance in our heart concerning a matter. Otherwise we have unrest, uncertainty, or agitation.

We know better than to argue with an umpire in a ball game. He has the last word. Either we're safe or we're out. To argue with the umpire may get us thrown out of the game. The peace of God is the umpire who calls the strikes and causes us to know whether we're on safe ground or in error. What is the nature of this peace? How do we know when we have it? Are there conditions for having it?

There most certainly are. Unless we meet certain conditions we can't know the peace of God and consequently we're in great danger of missing God's guidance for our lives.

The peace of God is *not* a mere absence of disturbance around us.

"Oh, it's these miserable circumstances around us," we complain. "The rent is due, the children are sick, and the neighbors are nasty. My boss is grumpy and somebody stole the hubcaps off my car. No wonder I don't have any peace."

The ones who march for peace say, "Oh, if we could just have another government, end the war in Vietnam, and ban everything that causes pollution. That would bring peace."

But the peace of God isn't dependent upon circumstances. It is a state of being that originates within us. We are conscious of being at rest, at peace, regardless of the circumstances around us.

Jesus was in the boat with the disciples in the middle of the Sea of Galilee when a storm blew up. The waves were bursting over the sides and the disciples were frightened, but Jesus was sleeping soundly in the back of the boat.

"Master, master, don't you care that we perish?" they shouted as they woke him.

Jesus said, "Everything is all right."

"But Lord, You don't understand the circumstances—look at those waves!" the disciples moaned.

Confidently, He arose and spoke to the waves. He had the peace of God within. No waves, regardless of their size, could upset Him.

One day I was driving my car on an ice-covered road. Suddenly the car started sliding. I saw telephone poles and guardrails looming up ahead. Yet inside me was that strange peace telling me, "Everything is all right, Bob, don't panic. I have My hand on the wheel." And praise the Lord, He did. After two and a half spins my car stopped, facing the guardrail without a scratch.

His peace is more than coming home from work and finding everything quiet and calm, the kids playing peacefully, your wife in perfect harmony. No, the peace of God can be with you even when you come home tired, the children are fighting over a toy, the television is going full blast, and your wife has burned the dinner. His peace inside of you makes everything all right.

There is an old story of a group of artists who were asked to paint a picture of peace. Each chose a different scene. One painted a sunset. Another the quiet ocean. A third a harvest scene. But one painted a picture of a roaring waterfall and just above the thundering water he painted a little bird sitting on a slender branch, its head under its wing, asleep. The bird sits peacefully on the branch. Doesn't she hear that roaring fall just below? Sure, but the roar can't touch her. She has wings.

The peace of God is a supernatural rest in the midst of surrounding unrest. To wait for circumstances to change so we can have peace could mean waiting forever. Circumstances won't really change until first *we* are changed.

In Phil. 4:6–7 Paul gives us a condition for this peace and also tells us something of its nature: "Don't worry over anything whatever; tell God every detail of your needs in earnest and thankful prayer, and the peace of God, which transcends human understanding, will keep constant guard over your hearts and minds as they rest in Christ Jesus" (Phillips). The peace of God *transcends* human understanding. We may question ourselves, even our own understanding; our friends and neighbors may say, "How can he be so peaceful when he just lost his job and his wife is in the hospital?" but that's what the peace of God does, transcending all understanding (and misunderstandings, I might add).

The peace of God *guards* our hearts and minds as they rest in Christ Jesus for it is in these areas (our emotions and intellect) that we are most susceptible to false guidance. When my emotions or intellect are upset, I know to be on my guard.

I was speeding down a country highway late one night when without explanation my "peace within" was disturbed. Something in my mind began to go click . . . click . . . click. Something was wrong. I slowed down.

"What is it, Lord?" I asked. "My peace has been disturbed."

Softly, in my spirit, I sensed a warning: "Watch out for deer!" Having become accustomed to listening to the kind of guidance that comes from a disturbance of the peace within, I simply said, "Thank You, Lord," and slowed down.

Rounding the next bend, my headlights suddenly picked up the form of a large doe standing beside the road. Startled, she leaped—right in front of the car. But since I had been forewarned, I was able to stop in time without hitting her. I had been prepared by a form of guidance that is not often recognized.

The peace *of* God cannot be ours unless we have made peace *with* God. And peace with God can come only through our repentance and confession followed by God's forgiveness. For instance, if someone had committed adultery five years ago and in order to keep it hidden had mentally suppressed it, it would be impossible for him to know peace *with* God. How could he know the peace of God with something like that tearing the insides out of him night and day?

If we confess our sins, God is just and forgives. That's a definite promise. However, we are required to open up all hidden sins, which is often a frightening experience. Yet how wonderful it is to have everything cleaned up between us and the Lord Jesus Christ.

Our *behavior and attitudes* affect our peace with God. There is an admonition and warning to husbands in I Pet. 3:7: "You husbands should try to understand the wives you live with, honoring them as physically weaker, yet equally heirs with you of the grace of life. If you don't do this, you will find it impossible to pray properly" (Phillips). Peter's principle, of course, applies not only to husbands in their relationship with their wives, but to every other relationship as well. You cannot know the guidance or sense the leading of the Spirit when you have a *turmoil* inside. Turmoil is like the tinfoil dropped by enemy planes—it jams our spiritual radar.

Many people who come to me for counseling and prayer are all worked up inside. Discovering this, I say, "All right, come on, out with it. I know there is something hidden in your life, an unsettled matter between you and God." Even if the disturbance is manifested by a bad relationship with another person, I know it is still *caused* (remember the difference between symptoms and causes?) by some short circuit with God.

We cannot know the peace of God if we are *disobedient* to His law. Isaiah says: "Oh, that thou hadst hearkened to my commandments! Then had thy peace been like a river, and thy righteousness like the waves of the sea" (Isa. 48:18). Verse 22 reads: "There is no peace, saith the Lord, unto the wicked."

Love is another condition for peace. The psalmist sings, "Great peace have they who *love* thy law, and nothing shall offend them" (Psa. 119:165). If we are filled with God's Spirit, live in His Spirit, and walk in that Spirit, we are guaranteed the continuous presence of God's peace in our hearts.

Peace *with* God will bring the peace *of* God until it settles your nerves, fills your mind, floods over your spirit, and in the midst of uproar around you gives you the assurance that everything is all right. You can have it in the kitchen with pots boiling over and guests coming for dinner. It can be yours on the front lines with guns going off over your head. You can claim it on the freeway with cars piling up on all sides, knowing you're going to be late for an important appointment. The peace of God guards your heart and mind, and you rest in Jesus Christ. People who know the peace of God don't take tranquilizers. He is their tranquilizer.

Peace within is our key to this basic form of guidance. When you know the peace of God, you will find the leading of the Spirit quite accurate and very precise. Guidance coming as the peace of God literally arbitrates and settles the disputes in our hearts and minds concerning specific actions.

Can you depend on an inner *voice* alone to settle a matter

in which you need guidance? In the midst of an argument with yourself you say, "Lord, You know I'm willing to give my rent-money to this urgent cause if that's what You desire." Suddenly there is the peace of God inside. No more churning, no more stirred-up feelings. "Sure I'll give my rent-money. The Lord will provide."

A carpenter friend of mine received an urgent call from a missionary in South America. The mission needed someone to build a church structure. The carpenter was being asked to quit his job in the States and come down and help. There's good biblical authority for such a call. In fact, it was in answer to such a call that Paul left Asia and went to Macedonia. The carpenter had two of the harbor lights in line —the objective standard (God's Word) and the circumstances (divine providence). But the middle harbor light, the inner witness of the Holy Spirit (the peace of God), was missing. He prayed, "Lord, I'm willing to go." But still there was no peace, just an urgent unrest inside.

Some people mistake that urgent unrest as a call from God. They are often led far astray, with tragic consequences. God may speak suddenly, causing a stirring in your spirit; but He very seldom requires you to do anything until you've recognized His peace and assurance about the matter.

In this particular case, the peace never did come, and the carpenter wisely concluded that God did not want him to go to South America. His refusal to go meant the church structure could not be built. Yet time proved he was right, for in less than a year an earthslide destroyed every existing building in that region. It was only then that the carpenter received the peace of God to go—and he went.

Another friend of mine was enroute to the Philippine Islands. He stopped in San Francisco to purchase a tape recorder. He was attracted to a machine costing $300. However, he only had $320 to spend for the entire trip. Inside he heard a voice say, "Buy that recorder."

"But Lord," he argued, "I can get a tape recorder for $50!" He walked around the store looking at cheaper models, but the guidance was too strong to dismiss. Returning to the expensive machine he said, "Lord, you know I'm willing, but I've got to know this guidance is from You." Suddenly there was a peace within, and my friend purchased the expensive machine. Arriving in the Philippines he discovered that the electrical current in the Islands fluctuates. His new recorder had a built-in stabilizer. Had he bought a cheaper one, he wouldn't have been able to use it.

The peace of God was the umpire, the deciding factor.

Unless you know peace *with* God and the peace *of* God, divine guidance can never become perfected in your life. Peace is the deciding factor, because it is the one thing Satan cannot imitate or counterfeit. Satan can imitate the voice of God. He can speak through prophecy, signs, visions, dreams, revelations. He can even counterfeit love and goodness and appear as an angel of light. But he *cannot* imitate the peace of God.

When Jesus sent his twelve disciples out to preach the gospel, he gave them authority to expel evil spirits and heal all kinds of diseases. He also gave them some sound advice: "Wherever you go . . . find . . . someone who is respected, and stay with him until you leave. As you enter his house give it your blessing. If the house deserves it, the peace of your blessing will come to it. But if it doesn't, your peace will return to you" (Matt. 10:11–13 Phillips).

Jesus told his disciples to greet a house upon entering. Almost every one of the letter writers in the New Testament followed this advice, even in their writing, as they started with the greeting, "May grace and peace be unto you from God the Father and his son, Jesus Christ."

This was not a mere formality. When Jesus walked into a room He said, "Peace be unto you," and I don't think He was merely being polite. Something happened in a room when He spoke those words; something of the same nature as when He spoke and the stormy waters were calmed. Nervous minds and hearts were calmed at His words.

In the name of Jesus I have gone into homes and said, "Peace be unto you," and immediately sensed something was wrong. That little clicker inside me went off: click . . . click . . . click. I would look around—a picture of Jesus was hanging on the wall, Bibles were here and there. It looked like a spiritual household. But inside me the umpire was saying: "Watch out! Be careful! Walk softly! There's something in this house that isn't receptive to the peace of God."

Once, driving down the highway, I was listening to a radio preacher: "You need to know Jesus. Salvation is in following Jesus," he said. It sounded good, but inside me the little warning signal went off. Click . . . click . . . click. "Watch out, something is wrong," it said. I argued with the umpire: "I'll just hear this man out; he sounds good enough." But when I came to the end of the program the announcer revealed that the program originated from a source which denies the deity of Christ. The words had sounded good enough, but the umpire within had warned. That man wasn't speaking truth because he represented a group which doesn't believe the whole counsel of God.

The peace of God is the umpire within us, guarding us against slipping into wrong action or false doctrines.

CHAPTER

11

SURROUNDED BY CIRCUMSTANCES!

Our outward lives are a continuous unfolding of circumstances, and most of us have particular ways of interpreting them. If the Dow-Jones index is up and we make $500 on the stock market we say, "God is making everything work out right for me." But if the roof leaks, the car breaks down, or we lose our last penny in the stock market we might say, "*Under* the circumstances I guess I'm all right, but the devil sure is giving me a hard time."

In reply to this the New Testament asks the question, "What are you doing *under* the circumstances?" Paul says in Romans, "All who will take God's gift of forgiveness and approval are kings of life" (Rom. 5:17 *Living Letters*). We are designed to live above the circumstances.

We've already discussed how God uses circumstances to guide us whether we're aware of it or not, and how He allows adverse circumstances to crowd us back into His will. Once we've committed our lives, God is in complete control of every circumstance in our lives, good *and* bad. If Satan gets in a lick or two, it is only because God has allowed it, not because He isn't looking. The Bible specifically promises that for those who love God all things work together for good (Rom. 8:28). Mark it down that this refers to *all* things.

Remember the three harbor lights of guidance? They are: the written word of God (objective standard), the Holy Spirit (subjective witness), and circumstances (the providence of God). It is to this last light, God's use of circumstances in direct, conscious guidance, that we now look.

It is possible to read the Word of God out of context and therefore be misled. What we may understand to be the Holy Spirit speaking can be equally misleading unless the peace of God is present and the leading conforms to the Word of God. Likewise, circumstances taken apart from the other two can lead us even farther astray. Circumstances can be misinterpreted in one of four basic ways according to our predisposition:

1. "God is putting me through a test."
2. "I'm being punished for my disobedience."
3. "The devil is after me."
4. "I'm being persecuted for righteousness' sake."

Most of us are more easily swayed by circumstances than by anything else. After all, circumstances are visible and seem very real. Anything that touches us outwardly is circumstance: cold, heat, hunger, pain, etc. If we want to grow up into mature sons and daughters of God, guided by His Holy Spirit, we must allow God to break us of vulnerability to circumstances. We *can* learn to discern God's hand in circumstances in positive or negative guidance, but we must *also* learn that favorable or unfavorable circumstances cannot be taken alone as a sign that we are in or out of the will of God.

Recall the story in Numbers 22 concerning Balaam who was bribed to prophesy against the children of Israel. God set a series of circumstances into action to prevent Balaam from going against His will: the rebellious donkey, the narrow place where the donkey crushed Balaam's foot, the angel with the drawn sword, and ultimately the angel who said, "Surely now also I had slain thee."

Balaam wasn't looking for guidance. He *knew* he was going against God's will and refused to pay any attention. But God *did* arrange a set of negative circumstances to stop him. Spiritually, this principle is known as divine resistance. As a person or a group of persons insists on going their own way God turns up His rheostat, resisting the people from going in their own way, a way which will result in self-destruction.

The Holy Spirit had Hosea warn Israel that continued persistence in her own way would result in the increase of the intensity of God's corrective measures. It is important for us to know God will arrange a set of negative circumstances to stop us when we are going against His will. The increase of the severity of the circumstances seems to be in proportion to our continued rebellion.

An impulsive young Christian often became upset at home and took his car and drove downtown to witness for Christ on a street corner. He avoided doing chores by telling his parents, "I'm going out to work for the Lord."

One day he prayed, "Lord, teach me to walk in your will." Soon afterward, something happened to upset him, and he ran out to his car to go downtown "for the Lord." But the car wouldn't start. There seemed to be nothing mechanically wrong, it just wouldn't start. He finally gave up, went back in the house, and forced himself to remain calm.

That night as the family started out for church, he got into his car, turned the key in the ignition, and it started immediately. He was mystified. A few days later it happened again. The young man became upset at home, ran to the car, and it refused to start. Yet when the family went someplace later, the car started like a dream.

After three or four times the young man became suspicious. Once he went out in the morning just to test-start the car. It started right up and ran smoothly. Yet later that day, when he felt restless and wanted to go for a ride, it wouldn't start at all. At last he prayed, "Lord, what's wrong with my car."

The answer was clear: "You wanted to learn how to walk in My will? I've kept you from going your own way."

He could only say, "Thank You, Lord!"

God has the power to make your car stop or run. If you're *not* certain whether you're moving in or out of His will, then pay attention to circumstances like that. A flat tire. Missing the plane at the airport. The house you thought God wanted you to buy which was sold right from under your nose. If God had wanted you there on time or wanted you in that house, no circumstances could have prevented it from happening. So thank the Lord for *all* circumstances and learn to look for and recognize His guiding hand.

God also uses circumstances to *confirm* His guidance. The word of God came to Jeremiah and said, "Behold, Hanameel, the son of Shallum thine uncle shall come unto thee, saying, Buy thee my field that is in Anathoth; for the right of redemption is thine to buy it" (Jer. 32:6–7).

Here are two of the harbor lights of guidance lined up: God speaking directly to Jeremiah by His Spirit in accordance with God's written Word (the reference to the right of one relative to buy or redeem land from another). From a natural, logical point of view, still, it looked like a pretty ridiculous proposition because the word came while the prophet was a prisoner, and the land he was told to buy was at the time occupied by the army of Nebuchadnezzar who was holding Jerusalem under a siege. Furthermore, Jeremiah knew the outcome of the siege. He knew he and all his people would be taken as captives to Babylon. He did know, however, that one day the land would be returned to the children of Judah.

Reading on we find: "So Hanameel mine uncle's son came to me in the court of the prison according to the word of the Lord, and said unto me, Buy my field, I pray thee, that is in Anathoth which is in the country of Benjamin: for the right of inheritance is thine, and the redemption is thine; buy it for thyself." Jeremiah said, *"Then I knew that this was the word of the Lord,"* and he bought the field (Jer. 32:8).

Experience had taught Jeremiah that even when God spoke to him and the word was confirmed by the written Law, he shouldn't make a move or conclude that God Himself had spoken *until* he saw the circumstances fall into place. Once he *knew* this was guidance from God, he bought the field and didn't worry about the army of occupation who happened to be camped there—nor about his own imprisonment and impending captivity.

Once we are sure our leading is from the Lord it is time to drive down our stakes and not permit anything or anyone to lead us away. Failure to obey clear guidance leads to compromise. Once the three harbor lights line up, we must keep a straight course regardless of doubts or feelings.

During World War II, Navy destroyers operating in enemy waters were given definite compass headings by the group flagship. Under no circumstances were they to alter their course. Immediately afterward, a low-flying airplane spread a thick smoke screen just ahead of them. They plowed into the dense smoke, but the blinding circumstances did not deter the various captains because they had received clear instructions. If one of the captains had doubted the initial orders, begun to get nervous and felt like he should change his course, he would have immediately endangered his own and the other ships.

Once guidance is clearly given by the Lord, confirmed by witnesses, and established in your heart, you can expect a Satanic smoke screen of confusing voices and circumstances to surround your frail vessel. Remember, steady-as-she-goes, for the course has been set. As we sail on in faith and obedience to our initial guidance, the end is guaranteed. On the other side of the smoke screen is clear sunlight.

When you married, were you sure that girl was the one God wanted you to have? Then hold to the initial leading, remembering even perfect marriages have their ups and downs in the smoke screens of life.

So now you're in school, struggling with finances. Circumstances demand that you live in a tiny apartment, and each time you try to study the baby cries. Every time you try to communicate, it ends in an argument, and you say, "It couldn't have been the Lord who brought us together. We're both so miserable."

Now if you were sure of your initial leading, then remember your marriage vows: in sickness and health, rich and poor, good or bad *circumstances.*

In the days preceding my graduation from college I was becoming anxious over my direction in life. Most of my other classmates knew exactly what they were supposed to do, but I was still waiting for God to direct me. Even though I wanted to go to the mission field as a minister, there was an increasing awareness that the Holy Spirit was directing me toward a new interest in medicine. As the witness built within, God directed me to Heb. 10:5, which said, ". . . sacrifice and offering thou wouldest not, but a body hast thou prepared me." This was the objective standard of my commitment to do the will of God. Two of the three harbor lights had fallen into place (even though my *desires* were to go in a different direction).

Then, on the day of graduation someone stuck a pamphlet in my hand. I looked at it and it was like a serpent. It was a pamphlet promoting a medical school. With all my heart I wanted to be a minister, but now the third harbor light had fallen in line. I knew what I must do. Going home I fell on my knees.

"Lord," I prayed, "I'd rather be a minister, but if this is where You want me, I'll go." At that moment the peace of God swept over me, and I knew God was speaking. All the lights were in focus. My initial guidance was sure.

My wife and I arrived at the school and found the pamphlet had greatly misrepresented the facts. The students worked eight, sometimes twelve, hours a day. Besides, we had to pay the school for the privilege of working. We wanted to leave right away, but the Lord said, "Did I not bring you here?"

I said, "Yes, Lord."

Circumstances were seeking to dictate to us. Every day we mentally packed our bags to leave. Several times we literally packed only to have to unpack later. We knew our initial leading was correct according to the harbor lights. It was the only thing that kept us from panic and making a costly mistake.

The conflict within and without became almost unbearable. Finally we said, "God, you brought us here and the only way we'll leave is for them to carry us out feet first." That ended the conflicts. Vacillation was replaced by genuine spiritual victory and peace in the midst of unfavorable circumstances. We both graduated with honors.

This same principle held true in the lives of the disciples.

In the story of Jesus on the stormy sea as related in Mark 4:35–38, Jesus had spoken to the disciples saying, "Let us pass over unto the other side." However, Jesus fell asleep and soon a mighty storm broke over the boat. The disciples were afraid. The waves were breaking into the boat and it was filling with water.

These events compounded a frightening circumstance, and if the disciples hadn't remembered their initial leading, they would most likely have come to the conclusion that they were out of the will of God in a storm-tossed boat. But Jesus *had said*, "Let us pass over to the other side." *That* was the leading. No waves should cause them to turn back —and none did.

The devil attacks many people by causing them to lose sight of their initial leading and become vulnerable to circumstances and impulses. Once we know where God is guiding, no matter what happens—hard times, suffering, poverty—we can *know* we are where God wants us.

If you ever lose sight of that initial leading, confusion will follow. If you begin to ask, "Should I have come here in the first place?" you might as well leave. If you don't know that God brought you, there is no foundation for any further leading.

Perhaps a man is asked to teach Sunday school. He prays, "Lord, do *You* want me to teach?"

"Yes, I want you to teach," comes the answer. Now if God wants you to teach, and you know that, then you can take anything from the superintendent. Buckle down, stay with it, hold your initial leading.

When the storm comes, Jesus will get the boat through. Are you in stormy waters with your husband or your wife? Your boss? Your finances? Know your leading and place confidence in God's ability to complete that which *He* began.

The Israelites were led out of Egypt, and the Lord promised to guide them to Canaan. But they lost their initial leading. They doubted that God was with them, doubted that He would give them the promised land. They lost their way and wandered through the wilderness, tossed about by circumstances.

We must learn that *unfavorable* circumstances don't necessarily mean that we are *out* of God's will. Likewise we must learn that favorable circumstances are not necessarily a sign of being *in* the will of God.

The word of God came to Jonah, for instance, and commanded him to go to Nineveh and cry against the wickedness of the city. But Jonah rebelled. He heard the word, he *knew* what God wanted, and he deliberately ran the other way. He intended to go to Tarshish to flee from the presence of the Lord. So he went down to Joppa and found *just* the ship, which "happened" to be ready to sail for Tarshish. He looked into his pocket and just happened to have the correct fare. Rejoicing in God's "provision of circumstance" alone, Jonah "knew" this was the will of God after all.

Imagine yourself in your study and suddenly the presence of the Lord says, "Arise, go to Los Angeles and cry out against the wickedness of that city!"

"Not me," you say; "I'm getting out of here. I'll go to New York and get lost among the teeming millions. The Lord will never find me." So you run to the train station and there just *happens* to be a train leaving for New York in ten minutes. The fare is $84.50 and you just *happen* to have the right amount. "Glory to God, this must be the Lord helping me to run away," you reason.

Yet something happened to the ship Jonah sailed on. And something will sooner or later happen to you on the way to New York, even though at first the circumstances were *favorable* enough to be misleading.

A series of favorable circumstances may cause you to imagine that God is leading you when He isn't. If someone falls in love with another man's wife and a series of favorable circumstances work out so that they are continually left alone together . . . Now wait a minute! Is that God?

Remember, circumstances alone do not provide reliable guidance. They must line up with the other two harbor lights. What does the Word of God say about falling in love with another man's wife? What about the Spirit of God? Can you commit adultery and still have the peace of God in your heart?

We are not supposed to ignore or overlook circumstances. They are always a factor in guidance. But we need to see them in the right perspective. They *never* override the Word and the peace of God.

CHAPTER

12

DESPISE NOT PROPHESYINGS!

Prophecy is one of the gifts of the Holy Spirit, given to the church for exhortation, edification, comfort, *and* guidance. In this study we are mainly concerned with the use of prophecy in personal guidance.

The prophets in the Old Testament foretold wars and famines, prosperity and victories. Isaiah foretold the birth, life, death, and resurrection of Jesus with amazing accuracy. We readily accept the fact that God spoke through the prophets of old, but find it harder to believe that He can speak to us today in the same way.

Prophecy is one of the charismas of the church. A charisma is loosely defined as a special endowment of the Holy Spirit coming upon an individual to enable him to *know, do,* or *speak* in God's behalf as inspired by the Spirit. Presently the charismatic renewal is affecting all denominations and peoples the world over. One of the marks of this present-day outpouring of the Holy Spirit is a restoration of the prophetic voice to the church. There is a distinct difference in the original language between the word translated "to preach" and the one translated "to prophesy." The implication of the word prophecy is: a supernatural endowment to speak, a knowledge in the speaker that the content of the utterance has not originated within his own understanding, and as an oracle of God he has become a present-day mouthpiece to make known to the contemporary church the will and purpose of the Almighty.

In the Book of Acts and letters to the young churches we find that prophets served along with apostles and teachers. "And God hath set some in the church, first apostles, secondarily prophets . . ." (I Cor. 12:28).

We know also that false prophets and the misuse of prophecy were rampant throughout the Bible and the history of the church. Because of their misuse of it, Paul found it necessary to carefully instruct the Corinthians in the use of prophecy. Apparently this gift, along with the gift of speaking in unknown tongues, had caused quite a controversy. Since a prophetic message often comes in an unknown tongue followed by interpretation, Paul discusses these two gifts together in chapter 14 of his first letter to them. We read: "Let the prophets speak two or three, and let the others judge. If anything be revealed to another that sitteth by, let the first hold his peace. For ye may all prophesy one by one, that all may learn, and all may be comforted. And the spirits of the prophets are subject to the prophets. For God is not the author of confusion but of peace, as in all churches of the saints" (I Cor. 14:29–33).

Several important aspects of the use of prophecy are pointed out here. First, the apostle lays down a ground rule for all guidance by prophecy: "Let the others judge!" Paul's rule of safety is never to receive a prophecy which contains guidance while alone. Others should always be present to judge because in guidance we cannot afford to make a mistake.

In Acts 11:27–30 we read: "During this period some prophets came down from Jerusalem to Antioch. One of them by the name of Agabus stood up and foretold by the Spirit that there was to be a great famine throughout the world. (This actually happened in the days of Claudius.) The disciples determined to send relief to the brothers in Judaea, each contributing as he was able. This they did, sending their contribution to the elders there personally through Barnabas and Saul" (Phillips). Several prophets came to Antioch. When one spoke, others were there to judge. The message was an important one and the disciples couldn't afford to make a mistake. Paul says to let the prophets speak.

There is a difference between the office of the prophet and the spirit, or gift, of prophecy. Paul says that obviously all aren't called to be prophets, but there is such a thing as a spirit of prophecy that may fall on the entire congregation. This means that you and I may prophesy at times. Paul goes on to give advice to would-be prophets: "The spirit of the prophet is subject to the prophet."

We discussed earlier the three sources of wisdom: the supernatural wisdom from above which is peaceable and pure, the supernatural wisdom from below which is urgent, compulsive, bringing discord and strife, and the third source of wisdom which is the human mind and emotions.

How do you and I learn to recognize the exact moment when God wants us to open our mouth and speak through prophecy, a message in tongues, or an interpretation? Over the years I've learned that the beginner usually experiences a physical exhilaration and quickening of the Holy Spirit in his body. Most often this is experienced as a heart-pounding or a sense of excited expectation. Often I have said in a group meeting, "Will the person whose heart is pounding please obey the Lord." This is enough reassurance for him to recognize that the pounding heart or the fluttering stomach is often a prompting from God.

However, an uncontrolled, compulsive message does not originate in God. The one who ministers and feels himself *carried away,* out of personal control, should begin to question the source and validity of what he is experiencing. The difference between the promptings of the Holy Spirit and the compulsion of other spirits (human or demonic) can be easily recognized. The Lord leads, draws, prompts . . . Satan or the human spirit is always demanding, compelling —they *push!*

As you mature in the use of the gifts and ministries of the Holy Spirit, you can expect that the exhilaration and physical sensation of the promptings of the Holy Spirit will diminish. You will learn how to respond in obedience to the gentle tugging of the Holy Spirit.

As stated, the misuse and abuse of prophecy has led many churches to abstain from the use of it. But today we are seeing a renewal of the use of the gifts of the Holy Spirit in all denominations of the Christian Church around the world. With this new emphasis comes a need to learn *how* to use these gifts properly.

Prophecy has two functions in personal guidance. One is *directive,* that is, it contains specific instructions about a course of action. This is the most common use of prophecy in guidance. The second is *impartive,* that is, by the laying on of hands and prophesying, the Holy Spirit imparts certain gifts or a specific calling to the believer. An example of this is found in I Tim. 4:14: "Neglect not the gift that is in thee, which was given thee by prophecy, with the laying on of the hands of the presbytery."

Modern-day Christians are too often forced to discover their calling or place in the body of Christ by trial and error, rather than by means designated in the New Testament. This brings unnecessary trials and not a few errors.

Prophecy is a supernatural form of guidance that can lead us into deception unless we learn to test the prophet and the prophecy. I have found nine distinct scriptural criteria for judging prophecy.

The Bible speaks of true and false prophets and gives us a criterion for testing them. In Deut. 18:20–22 we read: "But the prophet, who shall presume to speak a word in my name, which I have not commanded him to speak, or who shall speak in the name of other gods, even that prophet shall die. And if thou say in thine heart, *How shall we know* the word which the Lord hath not spoken? When a prophet speaketh in the name of the Lord, if the thing follow not, nor come to pass, that is the thing which the Lord hath not spoken, but the prophet hath spoken it presumptuously; thou shalt not be afraid of him."

An obvious criterion for the truth or falsehood of a prophecy, then, is its *fulfillment.* In late summer of 1970 an evangelist came to Seattle. He claimed to have received a prophecy from God that the entire city would be destroyed by an earthquake during the first week of October. The prophecy was repeated in meetings and over the radio. It eventually got coverage in the newspapers. Several Seattle families sold their property and headed out of the city.

The newspapers carried the story of one husband who refused to take the prophet seriously. One day he returned home from work to find his wife and small children gone. He searched for months until he finally found them in another state, living in abject poverty and suffering from malnutrition, all as the result of their believing the false prophecy.

Seattle was not destroyed by earthquake during the first week of October, but the self-proclaimed prophet continues today undaunted, delivering new messages of impending disaster in meetings and over the radio. Gullible listeners continue to support this ministry with funds and take his prophetic words seriously.

A second factor is *accompanying conditions*. Most true prophecy in the realm of direction or foretelling is conditional. For example: "If you will take your place as a father and priest in your home the Lord will bless you and preserve your children." If we don't meet the conditions, we cannot blame the prophet or God when the blessing doesn't come to pass.

Obviously there are times when we cannot wait for the fulfillment to prove a prophecy right or wrong. We need to know immediately if a prophetic message comes that says, "Thus saith the Lord, your city shall be destroyed," or "There shall be famine in the land." It is obvious that the disciples at Antioch didn't wait for the famine to prove the prophecy. They acted upon it and sent supplies.

A third test or criterion is whether or not a prophecy is *scriptural*. If it is not in agreement with scripture, it is false. No guidance is valid unless it conforms in essence to the written Word of God.

A prophetic message saying, "Divorce your wife and marry another," is obviously coming from a wrong source.

A fourth test concerns the *public acknowledgment* of the word. A prophecy spoken to you in privacy or in secret implying that you should *not tell it to others*, is often false. Remember, Paul said, let *others judge*.

I have seen some sad results of this form of misused or false prophecy. One elderly widow in Florida was visited by a couple from the North who said the Lord had sent them to minister to her. They moved in. Every day the man would come forth with a prophetic utterance and his wife with an interpretation. The gist of all the messages was, "My daughter, as you share with these my servants, so shall you be blessed."

The widow gladly shared of her food and her money, until one day the message came, "Go sell your house and your possessions and give the money to my servants. Do not speak to anyone about this, and you shall be greatly blessed."

The widow loved her modest home, and that night, trembling with fear that the wrath of God might fall on her for her disobedience, she sneaked unseen to the house of a friend and told her what "the Lord had spoken." The friend brought her to a group of Christians who were able to show her in the scriptures that this kind of prophecy is false.

This is not an extreme or unusual example. Beware of anyone who has a "word from the Lord" to speak to you in private. A legitimate word of directive prophecy can come to you through a friend, but ask your friend to speak it openly where others can judge.

I knew a young woman who had been married for ten months when some other women in the church took her off in a corner and prophesied, "Thus saith the Lord, my daughter, you married out of My will. Thy marriage shall not last." The immediate result of this was an estrangement between the husband and wife, followed by several years of pure agony.

I knew nothing of the prophecy, and one day I happened to say to her, "Sometimes we get off in a corner and prophesy to one another and it creates havoc." Her eyes filled with tears and she told me what the women had prophesied.

"I never told anyone before," she said. "I thought it was God, and I was so ashamed. I've been torn with guilt and didn't know what to do."

I shared with her some of the ways to test prophecy. She

realized the message she had heard and suffered from for so long was not from God, but from an earthly, sensual, or demonic source. God gave her a wonderful release and healed her life and marriage.

A fifth test of prophecy is that it should *confirm* something about which God has *already* spoken to you.

A couple in Texas felt a call to the mission field but weren't sure the guidance was from God. They had children, owned a prosperous business and a nice home, and didn't want to leave unless they knew for certain that God was calling. Hoping to find an answer, they traveled all the way across the United States to a camp meeting to seek the presence of the Lord. No one knew they were coming. They arrived after the meeting had begun, and just as they came in the door and started down the aisle a wiry little man jumped up and began to prophesy:

"Behold!" he cried. "Missionaries thou art and missionaries thou shalt be!" He had never seen the couple before. They now knew, beyond doubt, that God was speaking to them. This prophecy came as confirmation. They had already heard the word of God, other circumstances had fallen into place and now they saw the third harbor light of guidance line up: the Holy Spirit speaking confirmation through prophecy.

There is a sixth test of prophecy: Does it *witness* to your inner spirit?

There is a much misquoted verse of scripture, used most often by those who don't want to listen to the appointed teachers in the church: "But the anointing which ye have received of him abideth in you and ye need not that any man teach you: but as the same anointing teacheth you of all things, and is truth, and is no lie, and even as it hath taught you, ye shall abide in him" (I John 2:27).

John is talking about the Holy Spirit who abides in us and is our witness. How does He most often teach and guide us? By giving us an abiding peace about a matter, or a definite unrest. If the peace of God in our heart is upset by a prophetic message, we should exercise caution.

A seventh testing point concerns the *purity of the vessel.* The life of the prophet should agree with the prophecy. There are exceptions to this, and I have seen God use people who were living in open sin, people who were financially crooked or deceitful in other matters. But then, God also spoke truth through a donkey. Prophecy is a skill to be learned. Beginners always speak a mixture—part originating in God and the rest coming from the prophet's own human spirit. As we conform to Christ, the purity of our messages increases.

Learning to judge prophecy is also learning to judge the degree of mixture in a prophetic message, and to filter out the part that is from the human spirit. A look at the degree of purity in the life of a prophet often gives us an indication of the purity of his message.

An *eighth* touchstone in judging prophecy is the *spirit of the message* itself. John said, "For the testimony of Jesus is the spirit of prophecy" (Rev. 19:10).

All true prophecy should be in the spirit and character of Jesus, the sender. It is never harsh, critical, or condemning. It may often be a message of rebuke, judgment, or conviction, but it is always just and given in mercy. An excellent example is found in Matt. 23:37 where Jesus mourns over Jerusalem: "Oh, Jerusalem, Jerusalem! You murder the prophets and stone the messengers that are sent to you. How often have I longed to gather your children round me like a bird gathering her brood together under her wings— and you would never have it" (Phillips).

A friend of mine in Bible college decided he wanted to quit. He packed his bags in the middle of the night and left without telling anyone. A couple of weeks later, in a strange town and hungry for Christian fellowship, he sneaked into the back pew of a church. He was certain no one knew he was there.

Suddenly someone in the congregation stood up to prophesy. The gist of the message was, "Oh, thou who said in thine heart, I have hidden from God. The Lord sees and understands. You rebel fleeing from your calling, you cannot flee from God!"

My friend fell to his knees, repented, ran home to pack his bags, and returned to Bible college. This was a message of judgment and conviction, but it was tinged with mercy and not condemnation.

A ninth criterion for true prophecy is a discerning of *the burden of the Lord* in the message. This is difficult to define, but it should be present in all true prophecy. In Jeremiah we read of the prophets who tried to please the people by crying, "Peace! Peace! when there was no peace."

There are prophetic messages in which one hears and senses the longing of God and the heavy burden He feels for a straying or rebellious people. When this form of a message comes in a group meeting, the very spirit of it often makes the entire congregation break down and repent before the Lord. Such prophecy is never a message of condemnation, but rather of intense yearning, as when God spoke to Solomon in II Chron. 7:14: "If my people who are called by my name shall humble themselves and pray, and seek my face and turn from their wicked ways, then will I hear from heaven, and will forgive their sin, and will heal their land."

All nine criteria *may* be present in a true prophetic message although this is not always so. Never accept a message as truth, however, unless some combination of these several criteria is present.

Remember, prophecy can be received and enjoyed. Fear and danger of deception can be avoided if we keep in mind these nine criteria:

Fulfillment	Confirmation
Accompanying conditions met	Spiritual witness
	Purity of the vessel
Scriptural agreement	Spirit of the message
Judgment of others	Burden of the Lord

Evaluating prophecy and testing guidance should become second nature to us. Someone has said, "Open minds are like open windows; they need screens to keep the bugs out." We should not open our minds to prophecy until we know the message originates in God by the immediate application of the given criteria. We are responsible for what we receive. We should learn to discern the source.

A final word: Do not accept a prophecy on the basis of only one or two criteria. And then, even if you feel assured that the prophecy is true, do not accept guidance based on prophecy alone. Accept a prophecy only as *one* of the three harbor lights of guidance.

Misuse and abuse of the gift of prophecy have frightened many away from using it altogether. Paul urged the Corinthians, "Covet to prophesy," and told the Christians in Thessalonica, "Despise not prophesyings." But there must be a balance in prophecy. Some people give it *no* place, others give it *the* place, while God wants to give it *a* place in the life of the believer. In its proper place, prophecy is a tremendous tool in guidance.

CHAPTER

13

ANGELS, VISIONS, AND DREAMS

Angels, visions, and dreams are not the common, everyday form of guidance. Throughout the pages of the Bible we find these forms of guidance used only in moments of crisis or crucial importance, when it was necessary for God to make an impact and establish a strong point of reference, an unshakable initial leading.

An angel named Gabriel appeared to Mary and told her she was to become the mother of Jesus.

A host of angels appeared to the shepherds in the field and announced the good news of the Savior's birth. They instructed the shepherds to go to Bethlehem and told them where to find the child.

An angel was sent to Cornelius to give guidance to send for Peter to bring the message of life (Acts 10:1–5).

The Lord spoke to Ananias in a vision and told him to go to the house of Judas on the street called Straight and inquire there for a man named Saul of Tarsus, "for he prayeth, and hath seen in a vision a man named Ananias coming in, and putting his hand on him, that he might receive his sight" (Acts 9:11–12). Ananias didn't like the assignment and reminded the Lord of Saul's record: "How much evil he

126

hath done to thy saints at Jerusalem." But the Lord assured Ananias that Saul was a chosen vessel who would bear the name of the Lord before gentiles, kings, and the children of Israel. God spoke in a vision both to Ananias and to Saul because they needed a strong point of reference.

I've heard people say, "Oh, if God would only speak to me the way He spoke to Saul when He struck him down, blinded him with a terrible light, and spoke to him in a loud voice."

Why did God speak in such a spectacular way to Saul? Possibly there were two reasons. First, because Saul probably had been running from God's voice for some time. He had been a witness to the stoning of Stephen and was so stirred up by the gospel that he became an ardent persecutor of all who confessed the name of Jesus Christ. Saul wasn't lukewarm; he was in hot pursuit of the Christians. Yet at the same time the spirit of conviction was burning in his heart. God had to speak to Saul in a spectacular way because he was blind and deaf to the still, small voice of God. The *principle* is that the farther we are from God, the louder He may have to speak.

The second reason was the need for a strong point of reference in Saul's life, something he would never forget! God told Ananias in the vision, "For I will show him (Saul) how great things he must suffer for my name's sake." Paul was beaten, jailed, stoned, and left as dead for the sake of the gospel. But God had spoken to him in proportion to the degree of challenge he would face. Paul had dreams, visions, saw angels, heard voices, and was caught up into the third heaven. And he never forgot what happened to him on the road to Damascus.

What happens when someone has a vision, sees an angel, or has a dream? Often, the experience becomes an end in itself. It can become a trap for the Christian who may spend the next several years talking about it, rather than using the experience as a means to an end.

I krow a minister who had a vision twenty-five years ago. God spoke to him very distinctly. For twenty-five years the minister has preached the same vision. He has never moved beyond it.

Angels, visions, and dreams are scriptural forms of guidance, but if we make them an end instead of the means to the end, we have missed the point completely. Having dreams and visions and seeing angels are not necessarily a mark of spirituality. Paul stated the ultimate goal for us as Christians to be, "That I may know Him . . ." (Phil. 3:10). Our goal is to *know* Jesus Christ and to share His suffering and His resurrection, not necessarily to have three-hour visions, great dreams, or angelic visitors in our bedroom!

Insofar as angels, dreams, and visions are made subservient to the known scriptural goal, they are useful. These spectacular forms of guidance function as the scaffolding on a new building. But to become absorbed in the experience (scaffolding) and fail to build the building is a deception of the worst kind.

Angels *are* real. They appear throughout the Bible as messengers, guardians, and comforters. They minister to the saints, warn against danger, fight in battles, and will return in triumph with Jesus when He returns in Glory!

An angel opened the prison doors for the apostles in Jerusalem and told them to go to the Temple and preach the Word of God. Another angel awoke Peter when he was in prison and told him to arise and go. But are we to believe an angel if he comes to us?

Paul warned the Galatians, "But though we, or an angel from heaven, preach any other gospel unto you than that

which we have preached unto you, let him be accursed"
(Gal. 1:8).

Peter says angels are subject to the Word of God, and if
an angel speaks contrary to the written Word of God, he is a
false angel. Thus an angelic messenger must be treated like
any other avenue of guidance. We test the message as we
would test a prophecy or any other leading. The written
Word of God is the first criterion, but even if an angel
should give a message that we find in agreement with the
scriptures, the rule of the three harbor lights still stands.
The peace of God, and the circumstances must line up.

An angel may be a beautiful apparition and should he
come into our room might overwhelm us with his powerful
light and wisdom. But Paul reminds us that "Satan himself is
transformed into an angel of light" (II Cor. 11:14).

In the 13th chapter of I Kings there is the story of a man
of God who came from Judah to prophesy against the false
altar built by King Jeroboam. God had spoken to the man of
God, commanding him to return home to Judah without
eating or drinking. An old prophet heard what had happened, followed the man of God, and found him sitting
under an oak tree. He invited him to come home with him
and eat. The man of God refused the invitation, stating the
Lord had said he was forbidden to eat or drink. Then said
the old prophet, "I am a prophet also, as thou art; and an
angel spoke unto me by the word of the Lord, saying, Bring
him back with thee into thine house, that he may eat bread
and drink water. But he lied unto him" (I Kings 13:18).

The man of God believed the old prophet. He thought
the message of an angel *superseded* the Word of God. He
didn't know that the Word of God was binding.

Later, while they were eating at the table, the old
prophet finally spoke the truth and cried to the man of God

from Judah, "Forasmuch as thou hast disobeyed the mouth of the Lord, and hast not kept the commandment which the Lord thy God commanded thee, But camest back, and hast eaten bread and drunk water . . . thy carcase shall not come unto the sepulchre of thy fathers" (I Kings 13:21–22). Shaken, the man of God left for home and on the way a lion killed him.

Don't believe *just* because someone tells you an angel said it!

We are told in Acts 2:17 that prophecy, dreams, and visions are to be part of our Christian experience: "And it shall come to pass in the last days, saith God, I will pour out of my Spirit upon all flesh; and your sons and your daughters shall prophesy and your young men shall see visions, and your old men shall dream dreams." This is a quote from the prophet Joel, which, when quoted by Peter, takes on new meaning for the Christian.

A *vision* is a direct illumination from God and is often used as guidance in the Bible.

Twice in a row, Paul was hindered by the Holy Spirit when he tried to preach the word of God in Asia. Finally God sent a vision to Paul in the night: "There stood a man of Macedonia, [beseeching] him, and saying, Come over into Macedonia and help us. And after he had seen the vision, immediately we endeavored to go into Macedonia, assuredly gathering that the Lord had called us to preach the gospel unto them" (Acts 16:9–10).

Why such a spectacular form of guidance? Possibly God had spoken to Paul by the Holy Spirit earlier, but Paul hadn't quite understood. But also, Paul and Silas were to need a strong point of reference. The principle is that God must speak to us in direct proportion to the challenge we will face in the future. In Macedonia they went to Philippi and there they were badly beaten and thrown into jail. Had they gone to Philippi without being certain of their guidance, the circumstance of being beaten and thrown into jail might have caused them to doubt their leading.

Instead, deep in the inner prison with their feet fastened against the dungeon walls Paul and Silas prayed and sang praises to God until midnight. Suddenly an earthquake shook the foundations of the prison, all the doors were opened, and everyone's irons were loosed. Certain he had lost his prisoners, the jailer was about to throw himself against his sword when Paul shouted, "Don't harm yourself; we're all here."

The jailer was so amazed he cried out to Paul and Silas, "What must I do to be saved?" They told him and he accepted Jesus as his Savior. He then took the prisoners home, washed their wounds, and he and his entire family submitted themselves to water baptism that night as an outward sign of their belief.

What an amazing story! It teaches us the principle that when God sends a vision as guidance we may expect some adverse circumstances ahead.

A vision may be given to *prepare* us for a certain ministry. In Acts 10 we read about Peter who went up on the housetop to pray. There he had a vision. He saw something like a great sheet being lowered from heaven. In it were all kinds of beasts, creeping things, and birds—things Jews were not allowed to eat. A voice told Peter to rise, kill, and eat. But Peter refused, saying, "Lord, I have never eaten anything that is common or unclean." A third time the voice spoke to him saying, "What God hath cleansed, that call not thou common." Then the vision disappeared.

While Peter was wondering what all that meant, some men knocked on the door downstairs and asked for him.

They had been sent by Cornelius, a Roman centurion in the city of Caesarea. Cornelius had fasted and prayed until an angel from God told him to send for Peter. When Peter heard what the men had to say, he suddenly realized what the vision had been about. He went with the men to Cornelius's house where many gentiles were gathered to hear the Word of God.

Peter told them: "You all know that it is forbidden for a man who is a Jew to associate with, or even visit, a man of another nation. But God has shown me plainly that no man must be called 'common' or 'unclean.' That is why I came here . . . without objection" (Acts 10:28–29 Phillips).

God had prepared Peter for his ministry to the gentiles by giving him a strong point of reference. Later he was asked to explain his action to some of the disciples in Jerusalem who were full of criticism. When Peter told them of his vision and how it was confirmed in his experience with Cornelius, they had no further objection.

One day a dairyman in Southern California was in his room praying. Suddenly he saw a vision: Multitudes of businessmen were being swept into the kingdom of God. While the vision was taking place his wife came in and stood beside him. She began explaining to him simultaneously everything he saw, just as he saw it. It was a double witness. This man founded a fellowship of Holy Spirit filled businessmen which has grown to international stature. The vision became his strong point of reference in times of doubt and testing.

A vision can come as a warning of danger. During World War II a lady in England was sitting in church one Sunday morning. Suddenly she had a vision of the church being destroyed in an explosion. She jumped to her feet and told the congregation. The pastor decided to clear the church immediately. A short while later a bomb fell and destroyed the building.

Can a vision come from a source other than God? Of course, and it must be put to the *same* test as other forms of guidance. Is it scriptural? Does it reveal or impart knowledge and wisdom that is pure, peaceable, approachable? Or would it cause disharmony and rivalry? If so, it is not of God. In the name of Jesus Christ it should be refused.

A friend of mine was teaching in a home prayer meeting when suddenly he saw a clear vision of a large tin can standing on a shelf in a barn. Someone was putting pieces of silver into the can. My friend could see the picture in detail, down to a crooked nail on the shelf next to the can. The vision recurred three times, and at last my friend stopped teaching, looked at the group of people sitting around the room and said, "I don't know what this means, but I'm seeing someone putting away silver in a can. The Lord is telling me that the person is hoarding his money."

Across the room a man began to cry. "Oh, brother," he said, "I've been sitting here wondering if I was going to give that money to the Lord. I prayed and told the Lord that if you said anything about the money, I would."

He insisted that my friend go with him after the meeting. They went out to his barn where for years he had been secretly hiding his money (all in quarters and half-dollars) in a can on the shelf. My friend looked, and beside the can was the crooked nail.

The vision was a strong point of reference for the man who had been holding money back from his family for years. You may cheat your wife, your boss, or the government, but God sees your hidden treasure.

Dreams are not mentioned very often in the New Testament. They are frequently mentioned in the Old Testament, however. An angel appeared to Joseph in a dream, telling him that Mary was to become the mother of God's own son.

When the wise men had brought their gifts to the baby in the manger, they were warned in a dream not to report the whereabouts of the child to Herod. Again in a dream, Joseph was told to flee to Egypt, and in another dream he was told that Herod was dead and he could safely return with Mary and the child to Nazareth.

Dreams have a place in guidance, but take care; dreams can come from eating chocolate-covered dill pickles! I have a brother-in-law who is able to control his dreams in nightly series by what he eats prior to going to bed. Indigestion, tension, fear, and other pressures can cause some weird dreams. Put your dream to the test. If it is from God, it should pass the criteria for true guidance.

I've had two dreams in my life which I knew originated in God. I've had hundreds which did not! If a dream is of God, it is often meant to be a point of reference, a preparation for a time of testing.

Once I dreamt that I was walking through heavy brush and briars. They were pulling and tearing my clothes and skin. Finally I was through the thicket and discovered that before me was an insurmountable rock wall. I stood there in dazed helplessness and cried, "Oh Jesus! Help me!" Suddenly, off to my right, I discovered a small crevice just big enough for me to squeeze through. I struggled through the rock and on the other side was a beautiful blue expanse of clear water. I slipped down into the softness and suddenly it was as if I was in the arms of Jesus. I woke up in the morning praising God. I said, "Thank you, Jesus, for showing me that everything is going to be all right." *This* dream I knew was from the Lord.

For the next few months we went through some heavy briars and brush of trials and circumstances and finally, there it was, the insurmountable wall! I said, "Thank you for the mountain, Lord; now where is that crevice?" I *knew* in my heart it was there, and I just waited calmly for the Lord. Suddenly, there it was. I slipped through the crevice and into the beautiful blue water!

What if instead I had purchased a dream-book and looked up the symbolic meaning of "water" and "rocks"? Beware of such books as well as dream-interpreters, for they border on the realm of fortune-telling and the world of the psychic and often neglect or avoid God's Word.

God sent my dream to prepare me and protect me. I *could* have missed the point and opened myself wide to destructive wisdom from the Satanic realm. The result would have been confusion, and I could have "missed the mark" for my life and ministry.

Angels, visions, and dreams have their place in guidance, but only as they fall into line with the other criteria of guidance. We must take another look, for angels, visions, and dreams are only a means to the end: that we may know Christ and find our place in His Kingdom.

CHAPTER

14

SIGNS AND FLEECES

God often gives a visible sign as a symbol or token of something He wants us to understand. When Moses was watching sheep near Mount Horeb, God called to him out of the burning bush: "Go . . . and say [to the elders of Israel], The Lord God of your fathers, the God of Abraham, of Isaac, and of Jacob, appeared unto me . . . and said, I will bring you up out of the affliction of Egypt unto a land flowing with milk and honey" (Exod. 3:16–17).

Moses said, "But Lord, they won't believe me!"

To accommodate the unbelief of the Israelites, God gave Moses three *signs* to show them. First, the sign of the rod. Thrown on the ground, the rod would become a serpent. The serpent would become a rod again when Moses picked it up by the tail. Second, the sign of the hand. Moses would put his hand into his bosom and withdraw it. It would be leprous and white as snow. Again Moses would put his hand into his bosom and withdraw it. Now it would be restored and whole.

God told Moses: "If they will not believe you, or heed the voice of the first sign, they may believe the witness of the second sign. But if they will . . . not believe these two signs or heed your voice, you shall take some water of the river [Nile] and pour it upon the dry land; and the water . . . shall become blood" (Exod. 4:1–9 *Amplified Bible*).

Moses and Aaron went to Egypt and performed the signs God had given them. These were supernatural demonstrations that could not be performed by the natural power or ability of man. And the signs were given to generate faith.

We find three categories of signs in the Bible:

One, the *supernatural* working of wonders and miracles which are a demonstration of God's power in response to man's unbelief.

Two, the *allegorical* sign that foretells the nature of a coming event or judgment.

Three, a *natural* sign, such as the appearance of a star to signify that a promise or a prediction is about to be fulfilled.

The Lord commanded Isaiah to take off his robe and sandals and walk naked and barefoot for three years as a *sign* to the Egyptians and Ethiopians. This was to show how they would be led away captive, naked and barefoot, by the Assyrians.

In the same way, the Lord commanded the prophet Ezekiel to demonstrate the future captivity of the prince of Jerusalem in Babylon. Ezekiel was told to carry his baggage and cover his face as he walked in full sight of the Israelites —just as captives are made to walk without seeing the ground. The Lord said to Ezekiel, "For I have set thee as a *sign* unto the house of Israel" (Ezek. 12:6).

Ezekiel was instructed to tell the Israelites that he was carrying his baggage in their sight in such a way so that when they were carried away as captives they would recognize the hand of God in their misfortune and know that their captivity was a consequence of their rebellion.

We are told to watch for signs. Isaiah says, "Therefore the

Lord himself shall give you a *sign;* Behold, a virgin shall conceive, and bear a son, and shall call his name Immanuel" (Isa. 7:14). The shepherds in the field near Bethlehem were told of the birth of the child, and the angels said, "And this shall be a *sign* unto you; ye shall find the babe wrapped in swaddling clothes, lying in a manger" (Luke 2:12).

Jesus tells us, in Mark 16, that certain *signs* shall follow those who believe on Him: "In my name shall they cast out demons; they shall speak with new tongues; They shall take up serpents; and if they drink any deadly thing, it shall not hurt them; they shall lay hands on the sick and they shall recover" (Mark 16:17–18). In the Book of Acts, we see those signs did indeed follow the believers. And since Jesus is the same today as yesterday, and since his commands are timeless, we find the same signs still following the believers today.

Is it then scriptural to ask for a sign when we want to be certain that God is speaking to us? Here again, caution needs to be exercised. A sign *can* be a scriptural form of guidance, but it is never sufficient alone. The same rules for confirmation apply to signs as to the other forms of guidance. The sign must conform with the written Word of God, witness with the Peace of God in our heart and with the circumstances.

Jesus was often asked for signs. In Matt. 12:38–40 we read: "Then certain of the scribes and of the Pharisees answered, saying, Master, we would see a sign from thee. But he answered and said unto them, An evil and adulterous generation seeketh after a sign; and there shall *no sign* be given to it, but the *sign* of the prophet Jonas. For as Jonas was three days and three nights in the whale's belly; so shall the Son of man be three days and three nights in the heart of the earth." Thus when Jesus spent three days in the grave the Pharisees and the Scribes did not believe, although the *sign* had been given them.

Again and again we read in the Bible that many signs were given, but the people did not understand them. They were blind and deaf to the messages God was trying to convey.

There is often in us an inward disposition that blinds us to the truth, even when we see a clear sign. I once witnessed a remarkable healing. A woman had a large goiter on her neck and a man laid hands on her and prayed that God would take it away. Almost instantly, the goiter disappeared, leaving the skin hanging loose. My first reaction was one of unbelief: "That man must be a phony!" I said to myself. There was *in* me an unwillingness to believe, regardless of the evidence.

Likewise, I used to doubt the reality of the baptism in the Holy Spirit. I said, "If the Lord would ever permit me to pray in a new language, I'd *never* doubt the baptism of the Holy Spirit again." Later on I did pray in the Spirit and at the very moment I wondered, *Now is this the Lord, or am I just making it up?*

As long as there is an inward disposition not to believe, it makes no difference what God does or doesn't do in the way of signs. Jesus Christ performed wonders, signs, and miracles every day. Yet many who saw with their own eyes and heard with their own ears refused to believe.

When God gives us a sign, it is because He wants us to see something or do something. The first condition is that we be *willing* to be shown, even if it is something new and demanding. Even then, Jesus' word to the Scribes and Pharisees (and to Thomas who wanted to see the nailmarks in his hands) was that it is much better when we believe without a sign. Why is that? Because a sign can be faked. As mature

Christians we should walk in faith, not *following* signs. *The New Testament says the signs should follow us—not that we should follow the signs.*

Moses and Aaron performed signs to show the power of God. Pharaoh called in his magicians who were able to perform the very same signs. They threw down rods that turned into serpents, they copied the sign of leprosy and of water turning into blood. Satan can counterfeit every one of God's signs—which is one of the primary reasons all signs must be checked against the other harbor lights.

There is a warning in Deut. 13 against false prophets who may give a sign or a wonder: "And [if] the sign or the wonder *come to pass,* whereof he spake unto thee, saying, Let us go after other gods, which thou hast not known, and let us serve them; Thou shalt not hearken unto the words of that prophet . . ." (Deut. 13:2–3).

False prophets, then, also produce signs that will come to pass. Jesus tells us in Matt. 24:24, "For there shall arise false Christs, and false prophets, and shall shew great signs and wonders; insomuch that, if it were possible, they shall deceive the very elect."

The power behind these false signs is Satan himself: "Even him, whose coming is after the working of Satan with all power and signs and lying wonders" (II Thess. 2:9). Does that include the same kind of signs Jesus talked about in Mark 16? Healings, casting out of demons, and speaking in tongues? Yes, it does. These things can be and are being counterfeited by Satan. This is why biblical guidance is so necessary.

God wants to bring us beyond the point where we need signs to discern His guiding hand. Satan cannot counterfeit the peace of God or the love of God dwelling in us. When Christ's abiding presence becomes our guide, then guidance becomes an almost unconscious response to the gentle moving of His Holy Spirit within us.

But this is the ideal form of guidance, and there is often a great difference between the real and the ideal. Signs are given *to* us, because God meets us on the level where we operate. Signs are also given *through* us, to generate faith among unbelievers. As such, the signs and wonders are a fulfillment of God's promise in the scriptures. In guidance, when God shows us a sign, it doesn't mean we've received the final answer. A sign means we're on the way. On the highway we may pass a sign saying, "New York: 100 miles." The sign doesn't mean we've reached New York, but it tells us we're on the right road.

There is an amazing story of God's patience and willingness to accommodate our needs for signs and fleeces in Judges 6.

The scene opens with Gideon threshing wheat behind a winepress. Those were hard days for the Israelites. They had done evil in the sight of the Lord, and He had delivered them into the hands of their enemies the Midianites who had occupied their land for seven years and taken all their harvest. Gideon was doing the threshing behind the winepress to hide from the Midianites. Suddenly he was aware of an angel of the Lord sitting under an oak tree, watching him. The angel said, "The Lord is with thee, thou mighty man of valour."

Gideon retorted, "If the Lord be with us, why then is all this befallen us? and where be all his *miracles* which our fathers told us of, saying, Did not the Lord bring us up from Egypt? but now the Lord hath forsaken us, and delivered us into the hands of the Midianites" (Judg. 6:12–13). Gideon was a typical second-generation skeptic. He'd heard the big tales of what God had done in the old days. But where was the evidence now? Gideon's people were all living in caves and dens, hiding from the powerful enemy.

The angel had a message for Gideon. He told him the Lord wanted to send him to save Israel from the hand of the Midianities. At this, Gideon replied, "Oh, Lord, how can I deliver Israel? Behold, my clan is the poorest in Manasseh, and I am the least in my father's house" (Judg. 6:15 *Amplified Bible*).

The Lord said to him, "Surely I will be with you, and you shall smite the Midianites as one man!" (Judg. 6:16 *Amplified Bible*).

By now Gideon had begun to wonder what was going on. He said to the angel, "If now I have found favor in Your sight, then show me a sign that it is You who talks with me" (Judg. 6:17 *Amplified Bible*).

First God spoke by an angel, but Gideon wasn't satisfied. He wanted a sign and told the angel to wait while he went to prepare an offering. He returned with a sacrifice of meat and unleavened bread, and the angel told him to put the meat and bread on a rock and pour the broth from the meat over it. Then the angel reached out and touched the meat and the bread with the tip of his staff and fire flared up from the rock and consumed the meat and the bread. Thereafter, the angel vanished from Gideon's sight leaving him convinced. "Alas, O Lord God!" he said. "For now I have seen the Angel of the Lord face to face!" (Judg. 6:22 *Amplified Bible*).

Yet the very next day we see that doubt has entered Gideon. He has had to face some adverse circumstances and opposition from his own people and now he turns to God for additional assurance: "If You will deliver Israel by my hand *as You have said*, Behold I will put a fleece of wool on the threshing floor; if there is dew on the fleece only, and it is dry on all the ground, then I shall know that You will deliver Israel by my hand, *as You have said*" (Judg. 6:36–37 *Amplified Bible*).

Gideon already knew the will of God. He had seen the angel and the sign. He was convinced that God was the one who had said that He would deliver Israel by Gideon's hand. But he wasn't absolutely sure that God could do what He had promised to do. Gideon wanted more proof.

The next morning Gideon got up and checked the fleece. When he squeezed it, there was a whole bowl full of water. Now, surely, Gideon was reassured. But no, he turned right around and asked for another sign: "Let not your anger be kindled against me, and I will speak but this once; let me make trial only this once with the fleece, I pray; let it now be dry only upon the fleece, and upon all the ground let there be dew" (Judg. 6:39 *Amplified Bible*).

Gideon knew that he incurred the risk of divine displeasure by insisting on testing God when he already knew the answer. Gideon said, "Please, don't be angry God. I just want one more sign!"

In the next verse we see that God didn't get angry. In patience He accommodated Gideon's weakness and insecurity: "And God did so that night; for it was dry on the fleece only, and there was dew on all the ground" (Judg. 6:40 *Amplified Bible*).

Fleecing is a "popular" form of guidance with many, but if we read the story of Gideon there can be no doubt that the fleece was *not* a divinely ordained means of guidance. It was simply God's accommodation to the weakness of men. Not only that, but in all the scripture we find this method used only once.

Most of our "fleeces" are excuses for laziness or cowardice. We say, "I'll just put out a fleece. Lord, if you want me to go to work tomorrow, let the milkman put a quart of milk on my front porch instead of the usual half-gallon." Remember, God had already called Gideon. He knew Gideon's willingness. But most of us are unwilling and use the fleece method simply to rationalize away the requirements of obedience.

If you feel that you need to use a fleece for guidance, be sure you ask for one that requires supernatural intervention beyond the possibility of any natural circumstances. What we call fleeces are often not fleeces at all, but fall into the category of circumstances.

When Jonah ran from the presence of the Lord, we can imagine him saying, "Now Lord, if you want me to run away from you, just arrange to have a boat at Joppa ready to sail for Tarshish and I'll take that as a sign." That isn't a fleece, that is circumstance. We've learned what must always line up with the circumstances—the written Word of God, and the Holy Spirit giving us the peace of God.

Gideon knew the will of God beyond any doubt *before* he put out his fleeces. God accommodated him in his weakness because he was going to need an extraordinary point of reference. Gideon was required to meet the powerful army of the Midianites with only a handful of Israelites. God gave him sufficient signs so he wouldn't forget for a moment what God was able to do.

Gideon's experience is the exception, not the norm in guidance. Let it be understood that I know that in my spiritual youthfulness and immaturity, God has honored and does honor many things which we put out as a "fleece." If we *know* what God is asking of us and still insist on laying out fleeces, we may open ourselves to deception. Maturity demands that we learn to be guided by the Holy Spirit.

If I have a wife and meet another woman and fall in love, I may say, "Dear Lord, if you want me to have two wives, show me." It's in instances like this that the confused bigamist later testifies that he had an angelic visitor who told him, "Thus saith the Lord, thou shalt take two wives. You will be like Solomon, great in wisdom and with many wives!"

I have chosen an extreme example to bring home a point. I know people who are in doubt about a course of action and they "fleece" the Lord: "Lord, I don't know whether you want me to move to Florida or to California. The next time I go to the store I'll buy a bag of oranges, and if you want me to go to Florida, you let it be a bag of Florida oranges. If you want me to go to California, let it be a bag of California oranges."

Ridiculous! If you're in that kind of dilemma you ought to use the sanctified intellect Paul used when he set out to preach in Asia. He tried, but the Holy Spirit prevented him. If you don't know where to go, but you know you're not supposed to stay where you are, tell the Lord, "I want to do Your will. Therefore I'm going to start out in this direction and if You don't want me to go there, close that door, Lord, and show me another one." This is *circumstantial guidance* and it is scriptural.

The need for signs and fleeces arises from our unbelief. *God will accommodate us while we are in the process of learning to discern His will.* But counterfeit signs and answers to fleecing may deceive us, and we must learn never to take guidance from these evidences alone.

ONE STEP AT A TIME

We usually think that the more we learn to understand and practice the principles of guidance, the more confident and self-assured we will become. I've discovered, in practice, that the very opposite is true. The longer I walk with God, the less self-sufficient I become, and the more subjectively dependent I am upon God.

Now if that is the case, who wants to be guided?

Jesus said, "I am the vine, you are the branches, and unless you abide in me . . . you cannot bear fruit." The more we permit God to work in our life, the more He will strip us of the tendency we have to attempt spiritual fruitbearing on our own.

All of God's dealings in our life are designed to destroy our dependence upon ourselves. This is one of the reasons guidance must be a *step-by-step* proposition. If we could know all that is to happen, we would become cocky and forget our total dependence on God. Prov. 4:11 says: "I have taught you in the way of skillful and godly Wisdom [which is comprehensive insight into the ways and purposes of God]; I have led you in paths of uprightness" (*Amplified Bible*). God isn't talking to beginners here. He says, "I *have* taught you . . ." Now look at verse 12: "When you walk, your steps shall not be hampered . . ." (*Amplified Bible*). This Hebrew word for *walk* is better translated, *step by step*.

In Colombia, South America, the people walk to church meetings on narrow paths through the jungle. They carry a crude lamp made from a tin can with a candle in it, and by flickering candlelight they walk through the dark jungle, step by step.

I wouldn't like going through the jungle with that type of lamp. I prefer being able to see a puma or a boa constrictor far ahead of me. I want to be prepared. When I talk that way, what I am actually saying is, "I am really capable of handling *any* situation as long as I am properly prepared!"

When we walk with God, we learn that guidance is not given all at once. The Lord may say, "I want you to go into the insurance business."

"But Lord, what does the *future* hold?" you ask.

God says, "That's my business, don't you worry about it."

Maybe we have had a dream or heard a prophecy and feel we have *already* interpreted the future. This results in a false sense of assurance. Guidance, which has importance for the future, almost always comes in seed form. As a seed it unfolds one aspect at a time, and you will recognize it as it does. The daily outworking, however, is still a step-by-step walk in faith. When we are unable to plan the outcome, some of our self-dependence is destroyed, and we learn to depend more on God.

Psalm 119:105 says, "Thy word is a lamp unto my feet, and a light unto my path." Walk one step at a time, God is saying, with a flickering homemade lamp that doesn't light up the road three miles ahead like an electric sealed beam.

King Solomon was known for his wisdom, but in I Kings

3:7 he says, "O Lord, my God, I am but a lad [in wisdom and experience]; I know not how to go out [begin] or come in [finish]" (*Amplified Bible*).

This same Solomon said in Prov. 20:24, "Man's steps are ordered by the Lord; how can a man then understand his way?" (*Amplified Bible*).

The prophet Jeremiah cried out: "Oh, Lord, I know that the way of man is not in himself: it is not in man that walketh to direct his steps. O Lord, correct me, but with judgment; not in thine anger, lest thou bring me to nothing" (Jer. 10:23–24). Jeremiah knew the dealings of God.

When we have been taught the principles of walking with God it is necessary that we submit to this stripping of *self-dependence* and *self-determination*. If we don't, there is the possibility, as Jeremiah said, that we may be brought to nothing.

The goal is a childlike dependence on God, and the characteristics of one possessing a childlike spirit are that he is both *hungry* and *teachable*. Thus a mark of spiritual maturity is a childlike spirit! If that sounds like a contradiction, it is because we've developed a wrong philosophy of spiritual maturity. We think of the spiritually mature leader as one who is bold, confident, speaking with the voice of authority, making everyone tremble in fear and respect. This is our mental picture of the Apostle Paul.

Paul's picture of himself is a very different one. He writes to the Corinthians: "For I determined not to know any thing among you, save Jesus Christ, and him crucified. And I was with you in weakness, and in fear, and in much trembling. And my speech and my preaching was not with enticing words of man's wisdom, but in demonstration of the Spirit and of power" (I Cor. 2:3–4).

Is that how we want to be? That is where God wants us.

There have been periods in my ministry when everything was wonderful. The presence of God was real, and the Holy Spirit was doing wonderful things. There were visions and prophecies and it was simple to prepare for teaching. I thought, *Mumford, you are really moving with God!*

Suddenly everything slowed down. Instead of light and exuberant joy, there was just a drab gray: very few prophecies, no more visions, no more great teaching themes popping out each time I read the scriptures. What was wrong? Did I disobey? Had I backslid?

Finally I began to understand. Growing into maturity meant I must no longer base my relationship with God on *feelings*. FAITH is the key word in Christianity. By FAITH are we saved. By FAITH are we baptized in the Holy Spirit. By FAITH we are healed. By FAITH we are guided. We can never mature in our Christian experience as long as we depend on outward feelings and sensations. If *that* is our foundation, the whole building may come tumbling down one day.

It is essential that we allow God to strip us of our *dependency* on feelings. To accomplish that, God takes us through what may be called a *tunnel* experience. In the tunnel there is no feeling. It is dark all around and I say, "Lord, are you still with me?" No answer. But I do have my flickering candle-lamp. What does my Bible say?

"Thy Word is a lamp unto my feet, a light unto my path." So there it is, God's Word. I'm going to have to learn to trust God's Word, regardless of how I feel.

Jesus said, "I will never leave thee nor forsake thee." Even here in the long black tunnel where I don't feel His presence or hear His voice He's here!!

What if I panic? I've been in tunnels and panicked and found the Lord right next to me asking, "Did you call?"

"Yes, Lord. I just wanted to be sure You meant it when You said You wouldn't leave me."

"Of course, I'm here. I'll reconfirm My presence to you so you'll *feel* better."

But what happens now? The tunnel must be extended, because what God wanted to accomplish in my life was interrupted by my panic at the absence of feeling. The tunnel experience is designed to strip us of the outward and soulish dependency on emotionalism, which is anything but faith.

There are some who are unwilling to go through the tunnel. They panic halfway through: "Lord, please, I don't *feel* spiritual anymore; I want to feel you, Lord. I want to back out of this faith-walk."

There is no condemnation for those who want to remain on this side of the tunnel. But neither is there maturity. Paul scolded some New Testament Christians: "You're old enough to eat meat, but you're still drinking milk. When you ought to be teaching others, you're still being taught."

Once you come through the tunnel, there is new light on the other side, a deeper understanding of God's Word, a stronger faith, and with it, *responsibility* for what we've learned.

It is the same in guidance. Unless we're willing to be stripped of our dependence on outward signs and manifestations we will never be able to go on into maturity. Walking in mature obedience reduces the necessity for obvious guidance. That doesn't mean God no longer speaks to us in prophecy or through visions or angels or in an audible voice if *He* so chooses. *Being stripped of our dependency on feeling does not mean we will no longer feel God's presence.* It means we are no longer depending on it. Our mature faith is based on fact, not feeling.

Why can't we be exposed to more truth at a time? Why

can't God just show us the map and say, "This is where you're going to walk because this is what is going to happen"? God does not reveal all truth to us at one time because it would cause us to withdraw from total dependency on Him, and because knowledge of the truth makes us responsible for it. Both of these require a certain maturity which needs to be developed. Jesus told his disciples that there were things they simply couldn't bear to hear.

We are responsible for the truth we know. We are responsible for the guidance we receive. If we *know* the truth and *know* what God wants us to do, and if we deliberately ignore it or rebel against it, we're worse off than when we were ignorant. This is why we cannot become grown-up Christians overnight, even if we're totally yielded to God and willing to do everything for Him.

Maturity takes time. You can't get around that whatever you do. Sometimes we get excited and impatient saying we're not going to wait around for two or three years; we're going to grow up in two weeks! Oh, no, we won't. Let's not confuse the terms "mature" and "immature" with "perfect" and "imperfect." The child can be a perfect child although it isn't a mature adult. The immature flower bud is just as perfect as the full-blooming rose. The lamb is as perfect as the sheep. The only difference is the *time* factor.

The scripture speaks a great deal about sheep, lambs, and shepherds. We know Jesus as "the good shepherd," and He refers to believers as sheep and lambs. In John 10:27 Jesus said, "My sheep hear my voice," not, "My lambs hear my voice."

There is an illustration about two shepherds who let their flocks graze and drink water together. When it came time to part, one of the shepherds called for his sheep to follow him, and right away the sheep in his flock came out from among the others. The sheep knew their shepherd's voice. But what about the lambs? Why the lambs followed the sheep, of course.

When we're first born in Jesus' flock we are lambs, and we follow the sheep. Then, little by little, as we associate continuously with the shepherd, we begin to know His voice. By the time we are sheep, we're ready to follow Him and lead others along. The responsibility of the sheep is a grave one. When a sheep strays from the flock, lambs are apt to follow and get lost.

In the Christian community, the young Christians who cannot know God's voice yet, say, "Oh, I'll just listen to my pastor; he's mature in God." If that pastor isn't following the right directions, his flock will end up in the ditch. In God's plan, this is, as well, the role of the husband and father in a household. Tragedies occur and families are shipwrecked when the man in the house refuses to follow the guidance and direction of God so that he can lead his little flock.

Have you ever heard of the "Judas sheep" in the stockyards? When a new flock of sheep comes in to be slaughtered, the Judas sheep is let in among them in the pen. Specially trained, he soon wins their confidence and leads them toward the slaughterhouse. Just as they get to the gate, he jumps aside and the other sheep continue on to the slaughter. The responsibility of a sheep is an awesome one.

An unknown author wrote:

'Twas a sheep, not a lamb, that went astray
    in the parable the Lord Jesus told;
'Twas a grown-up sheep that wandered away
    from the ninety and nine in the fold.

And out on the hilltops and out in the cold,
   'Twas a sheep that the Good Shepherd sought.
And back to the flock, and back to the fold
   'Twas a sheep that the Good Shepherd brought.

Now why should the sheep be so carefully fed
   And cared for still today?
Because there is danger if they go wrong
   They will lead the lambs astray.

For the lambs will follow the sheep, you know,
   Wherever they wander, wherever they stray;
If the sheep go wrong, it will not be long
   Till the lambs are as wrong as they.

So still with the sheep we must earnestly plead,
   For the sake of the lambs today.
If the lambs are lost, what a terrible cost
   Some sheep will have to pay!

Pray that as a sheep you may lead the other sheep and the lambs to the shepherd. That, after all, is our objective—fellowship with the shepherd. God desires that we mature into sheep who know His voice. There are some who would rather be lambs all their life, just being fed and led, avoiding responsibility! But maturity is learning to feed yourself and in turn helping feed others. *Maturity is producing more than you consume.*

In our society we've been conditioned to think of maturity in terms of independence. Young people are told, "When you become mature, you can be independent."

Spiritual maturity is the very opposite. God doesn't tell us, "Now son, when you're grown and spiritually mature, you're on your own. You make your own decisions. You can choose your own vocation. You're old enough to have a life of your own and a home of your own."

Jesus said to Peter, "I assure you . . . when you were young, you girded yourself—put on your own belt—and you walked about wherever you pleased to go. But when you grow old you will stretch out your hands and someone else will put a girdle around you, and carry you where you do not wish to go" (John 21:18 *Amplified Bible*).

In my early ministry I was so full of zeal and eagerness that I went everywhere holding meetings. Jesus simply went with me. It was where *I* wanted to go. Then one memorable day when the Lord knew I was old enough, I rushed ahead to Pennsylvania . . . and Jesus stayed behind! There was the awful sense of His absence.

While we are yet young, Jesus goes with us through the most trying circumstances. He stays by our side even when we may be out of the expressed will of God, until one day— there's the drawing line! There's that voice *behind* you. (You've run so far ahead He's talking from *behind* you.)

"Young man, young lady, what's all the running for now?"

Then you begin looking around. Instead of just looking at yourself you say, "Oh Lord, I'm so sorry. Was there something *You* wanted me to do?" *There must come a time in our lives, if we are ever to become mature, when the initiative in our life passes from ourselves to God.*

Immaturity is going where *you* want to go; maturity is going where *God* wants you to go. It's that simple!

You say, "I think I'll go visit my sister today."

The Lord replies, "Not today. I want you to stay home today and fast."

"But Lord, I always visit my sister on Tuesdays."

"Yes, I know, but now you *go* at My bidding and you *stay*

home at My bidding. It is time for discipline. Now the time has come for you to begin to realize that I am King! I am giving the orders. Your Savior is now becoming your Lord!"

The ramifications of commitment to divine guidance, as understood in this book, produce a metamorphosis in the life of the believer. We pass from the bondage of a cocoon to the freedom of a butterfly by the process of death to the old and resurrection to the new. In divine guidance we go from a self-willed and sin-bound person to a new creature enjoying the full liberty of the mind of Christ and the ministry of the Holy Spirit. We have not been reduced to a mechanized robot. Guidance is not a bypassing of our personality; it is an enhancing of the moral freedom of a disciplined son who has learned to please his Father.

Stripped of *dependence* on feelings, desires, and the tyranny of human reasoning, we can walk in obedience. These are the things that have held us captive, and as we die to them, they are returned to us as our servants and not masters.

Once we were slaves to feelings; now we are free to enjoy them. Once we were slaves to inordinate desires; now our desires flow toward Him who promised that as we delight ourselves in Him He would grant us the desires of our heart. Once we were bound by the limitations of human understanding. Now in the resurrected Christ we are tapping the source of all truth, wisdom, and knowledge.

This is what Jesus meant when He said, "He who loses his life *for my sake,* will find it."

This is what Jesus Himself did, and this is what God the Father wants for us. This is how we become conformed to the image of God's Son who lives in our hearts by our faith.

Paul wrote to the Galatians, "I am crucified with Christ: nevertheless I *live;* yet not I, but Christ liveth in me: and the life which I now live in the flesh I live by the faith of the Son of God, who loved me, and gave Himself for me" (Gal. 2:20). The ultimate in divine guidance is when the Lord takes the initiative in your life and begins to move you toward His goal for you.

The passing of that initiative is your prerogative. God will not wrest it from you. You choose: "I give up the right to take the initiative in my own life, Lord. Here it is. Lead me." You daily confess: "My Father, thou art the guide of my youth" (Jer. 3:4).

King David perfectly described the fully guided life:

"The Lord is my *shepherd*. I shall not want. He maketh me to lie down in green pastures; He *leadeth* me beside the still waters.

"He restoreth my soul; He *leadeth* me in the paths of righteousness for His name's sake.

"Yea, though I *walk* through the valley of the shadow of death, I will fear no evil; for Thou art with me: Thy rod and Thy staff they comfort me.

"Thou preparest a table before me in the presence of mine enemies; Thou anointest my head with oil; my cup runneth over.

"Surely goodness and mercy shall *follow* me all the days of my life; and I will dwell in the house of the Lord forever" (Psa. 23).

Readers may write to:

> Bob Mumford
> P. O. Box V
> Ft. Lauderdale, Florida 33315

Be sure to read Bob Mumford's other book:

> *15 STEPS OUT*

And his booklet:

> *A PSALM FOR LIVING*

Available in bookstores or from:

> Logos International
> Plainfield, N. J. 07060